Investing in the Future

A Policy for the Next President

Investing in the Future: A Policy for the Next President

ISBN 13: 978-1466392205

ISBN 10: 1466392207

FIRST EDITION

October 2011

Other Books by Perry Jones

Poems and Dreams: A Sampler

The Book of Revelation

The Book of Revelation Workbook

Why Does God Allow Suffering?

Proof of the Existence of God

God's Plan for You

$300,000 A Day

Hyperspace Calculations

Investing in the Future

A Policy for the Next President

Investing in the Future

A Policy for the Next President

Investing in the Future

A Policy for the Next President

INTRODUCTION

This policy addresses issues which have stalemated and stymied the President, Congress, academicians and corporate and community leaders. I don't have all the answers and I expect you to provide the answers where I cannot. I feel the solutions I present here are workable, practical solutions for a variety of ailments which confront the American people and nation today. Many of these solutions will be controversial, and even if the people agree on them, they may be difficult to pass through a recalcitrant Congress.

I dedicate this Policy to God above, to you the people of the United States and to the men and women of our Armed Forces, especially to those who have fought and died on foreign shores throughout our history. Rest in peace, brothers and sisters.

6

JOBS AND THE ECONOMY

Capitalism has failed. It died as a result of the greed of big bankers and corporate CEO's. No, not all are guilty, but enough are, to force nearly 20% of the population of the greatest, richest nation on Earth into poverty. Jobs are dead. Millions are out of work. Millions who are working are struggling just to stay afloat. Many are trying to find second and third jobs so they will be able to put food on the table, buy soccer and softball uniforms for their children and pay the rent or mortgage. The millions of jobs we have lost are most likely gone for good. Some may return, but the vast majority of jobs which have fled overseas will remain overseas.

Rearranging Deck Chairs on the Titanic

The President calls cabinet meetings to discuss how to create jobs. Presidential candidates debate about who has the best plan to create the most jobs. Corporate leaders, economists, bankers, business owners and arm chair philosophers (I'll admit I am one), present proposals and entertain plans to produce the most jobs. What they all seem not to notice is that jobs are dead. We are like dinosaurs on the far side of the world the day after the asteroid has hit. We see strange clouds and lights in the sky; the ground rumbles and shakes; we know something is wrong, but eventually we are certain that things will return to normal. But they won't.

The economy is restructuring. None of the current field of Presidential candidates seems to understand this. No one in Congress seems to have grasped this. None of our corporate leaders or economists has recognized this. We cannot return to the economy of yesterday and the millions of jobs it created because the economy of yesterday no longer exists. It died a quiet death beneath the outrage of two wars, worldwide recessions and corporate debacles. The millions who are out of work are all hoping to find a job – to return to the consumer-based economics of a yesterday which is now nothing more than a fading memory. We can't get the jobs back because there are no jobs to bring back. We can't create more jobs because there are no more jobs to create. We may – possibly – create a few hundred thousand jobs – given enough time and fortuitous politics and a generous economy, but hoping for that is akin to hoping for the Palestinians to play nice with Israel. Sorry, it's not going to happen.

Any and all talk of creating jobs is useless speculation. It is a grasp at an idea that no longer exists. The jobs of the industrial era have gone the way of the whipmaker for the horse and buggy. They have succumbed to advancing technology. Trying old methods to create new jobs is nothing more than rearranging deck chairs on the Titanic. The orchestra may play soothing songs and the stewards may ooh and ahh over how neatly we have rearranged the chairs, but no one is taking notice that the whole ship is sinking! People, our jobs are gone and they are not coming back. Personally, I say good riddance. The people of China, Mexico and Asia can all do the work to produce the goods that will be of greater diversity and lower in price than if we had retained those jobs here. There may be exceptions. But to indulge in an exception is like jumping into a lifeboat from the deck of the Titanic only to clamber right back onboard again. We don't need jobs. We need work and there's a world of difference between the two.

"MADE IN AMERICA." Do you recall how proud we all used to be whenever we noticed that statement stamped into the bottom of some item we had just bought? We are even more proud today when we see those words. And we should be. The factories and businesses that can produce competitively priced goods at an equal or greater quality than the same goods produced overseas need our support. And rightly so. The American worker is the hardest working and most productive worker in the world. Our factories are the best. Our warehouses are the most efficient. Our distribution systems are the fastest and the most extensive reaching every city, town and hamlet in the United States. Let China choke on that!

The key to the label "Made In The USA" is productivity. Productivity is the result of efficiency. Efficiency is a product of speed and quality. Wherever we can compete in a world economy, we should compete. Whenever we can produce a superior product at a competitive price, we should. But such practices are the domain of the individual, the small business owner, the entrepreneur with a dream, not the football of Presidential candidates or state politics.

Alvin Toffler in his book "The Third Wave" identified three "waves" through which societies evolve. The first wave is the agricultural stage, in which humans gather into communities to farm and grow crops. The second wave is the industrial revolution which produced the belching smokestacks of thousands of assembly line factories around the world. The third wave is the technological era and we stand in the midst of that revolution today.

Computers, the internet and security cameras on street corners are some of the hallmarks of this third era. Toffler also indicates that political and commercial turmoil accompanies each wave. We can certainly see the truth of that. Because of this, any economic system we create must incorporate the technology and individuality which characterizes the Third Wave, and therein lies our key.

One of the characteristics of this Third Wave is that each individual has the potential to connect with any other individual anywhere in the world at any time of day. This means a direct communication is possible between those who wish to produce and those who wish to consume. No middle man is needed. No bulging factory is required. No huge drafty warehouse is necessary to hold thousands of items of product to distribute to eager customers. Today, each and every person has the potential to be both a producer and a consumer of the goods of the world. Alvin Toffler predicted just this occurrence in his book.

This bit of insight also reveals why the Post Office is failing. Emails, chat rooms, forums and groups have all taken the place of a paper trail passed through an extended organization. If that organization is to survive, it must streamline and reorient itself to the realities of today. Perhaps the Post Office can transform into an email provider, data warehouse, a cloud computing provider or web host. With this reorientation, snail mail could still be a function of the Post Office, but at a greatly reduced level of service than today. Maybe the Post Office should deliver mail only every other day and curtail service to some small communities requiring residents of said communities to pick up their mail at a central location. This is how the Post Office provided service to many communities in the 1950's. The Post Office should also perhaps raise its first class rate to $1.00 (Ouch!), but that would ensure that people use the Post Office only when it's absolutely necessary to do so, (and may eliminate a lot of junk mail!).

People are using the internet to connect with people half way around the world. Exchanging ideas, downloading music, watching videos, creating videos, posting photos are all part of the internet community. A current evolution is that some communities are now turning to the internet to schedule meetings and gatherings of like minded individuals in coffee shops and private homes. All these factors should provide a clue as to how the economics of tomorrow will differ from that of today.

Whether people work virtually over the internet or whether they use the internet to schedule a meeting with a potential customer, the economics of tomorrow is based on a face to face encounter. I can produce that instruction manual you need. You are a photographer and I need to schedule a wedding photographer. You have written an eBook that will streamline my business. The high schooler next door has created an app my daughter has downloaded to her smart phone. I have scheduled a web meeting with my accountant who lives a thousand miles away to discuss tax strategies for next year. My payroll is handled by an online service. My advertising agency provider has scheduled a web meeting with 5 of its representatives from cities around the world. The job of yesterday is dead, but there is plenty of work that needs to be done.

Have You Been Laid Off? Unemployment, God and You

If you have been laid off from work, maybe God wants you to be laid off. If you don't have a job, maybe God does not want you to have one.

I know you have bills to pay and food to put on the table. The rent or mortgage is due, the car insurance is due and you don't know where the money is coming from. For now, you may need to find any job that you can get but you also have to start trusting God.

I can tell you don't have faith in God because of several criteria God has established to measure that faith. Is your health perfect? Are you happy? Are your relationships perfectly supportive and loving? Do you own a business or have passive investments that provide you with the income you need to live the lifestyle you desire without having to work for a living?

If your answer to these questions is "No" then you have forgotten your relationship to God and you are living in sin. Before I go on, let me stop and say that I am just like you. Those who meet me may say that my relationships are not perfect, that I struggle with finances and my health could be better. But I now see where I need to be and God has led me to help others see that same place in their lives. By helping each other, we help ourselves as well.

We all think we know what sin is. We have heard it preached to us from pulpits and pastors, schools and teachers, parents and guardians of all kinds. But all that is incorrect. According to the Bible sin is when you do not live according to God's plan for you. Some people may think that God wants you to go to church every Sunday, obey the Ten Commandments, tithe, contribute your time to church committees and parental groups, or participate in bake sales or other activities at the church. That Could be true, if that's the plan God has for you - but it's unlikely.

God has set in each person's heart a certain dream that that person is supposed to fulfill. Along with that dream, God has given each person a talent or set of talents to help them accomplish that dream.

The talent God gave you may be singing or acting, driving a cab or boxing. It could be a doctor or nurse, dental assistant or customer service rep. You may be the next Rembrandt, Bach or Leonardo da Vinci. Or you could be Joe the Mechanic, Diane the pre-school teacher or Elaine the animal shelter volunteer. Following your path - that dream that God has given you - is called following the Kingdom of Heaven. What dream did God put in your heart? What would you do if you knew you could do anything and you knew you could not fail?

The problems in our lives, our neighborhoods and communities, our places of business, the schools and churches, in government, city, state and federal, between nations and peoples and with the environment are all a result of forgetting who we are. We are spiritual beings experiencing a physical existence. The divine spark of God lives in each mortal living thing, animating us, breathing us, living through us. When we cut off that connection to Spirit - to Source – to God - we grow ill, disconnected from the unlimited bounty which surrounds us, estranged from Him Whom We Should Serve. Our vision narrows until our focus is solely upon the cares and worries of this world - what bills to pay? how should we eat? what should we wear? where should we live? In this state, God becomes a distant Being we visit - if we visit at all - only once a week in some building.

That's not how it was meant to be. And maybe, just maybe the fact that you are out of work, or are struggling with health issues, relationship issues, drugs or addictions, unsatisfying work or financial issues is all supposed to be a wakeup call to you from God. Maybe, during this time of enforced time off from work, you should be focusing on God's plan for your life. Maybe God has a message for you, maybe there is something He is trying to tell you. Maybe there is something He wants you to do. And, while you have been so busy, busy, busy with your everyday, workaday life, you didn't take time off to listen to God on a daily basis. But now you can.

God speaks to everyone all the time. He always has. But we have been taught that He does not. We have been taught that He speaks only to certain people; pastors and rabbi's maybe, or prophets or evangelists. That's not true. God speaks to everyone all the time. God is speaking to you.

I do not know what God's plan is for you. But I do know He has one. I do not know what your innermost secret dream is, but I know you have that also - even if you have forgotten it - or even never knew it. You may have forgotten your secret dream over the years or suppressed it because it seemed childish or immature, unrealistic and people told you to grow up, be an adult, stop acting that way. And now you are an adult. But it is still there somewhere, dormant, lying there in your heart waiting to be reawakened, to be born again. It is waiting to come to life and empower you and all those around you and all those you meet. Living your dream will bring you unlimited happiness, prosperity, wealth, and joy. Living it is the only way to worship God. Not living it is to sin. How much sin are you in?

You will never be out of work if you put God's work first, you will never have to worry about your next paycheck when God is your boss. In this secular world, this may seem like a bunch of religious baloney, but it's not. God keeps His promises – even today. One promise is this: If you put God first, He will provide for all your needs – literally. With millions out of work, maybe with you out of work, you can and you will never have to worry about a job again. We need to get people back to work and God has work for you. I'm convinced that by doing God's work, you will never want for work, never worry about paying the bills, never have to fear about putting food on the table, never wonder where the next paycheck is coming from. God keeps His promises and He will keep His promise with you.

God wants you to be happy, to be full of joy, to live life fully and more abundantly, to experience exciting, supportive relationships, to be wealthy and prosperous. God says that His plan for you is greater than you can imagine. What is your dream? What is your secret mission? What is your true calling? What would you do if you knew you could not fail? What are your strengths? What are your skills? Therein lies your talents. And therein lies your dream - God's dream. What is your dream? This is where Community Training Centers come in.

Community Training Centers

"Failure is not an option," sings rapper Eminem, and we must get people back to work. But if the job of yesterday is dead, we must find a new way. We must integrate people into the new economy. The old industrial era schooling was fine for its day, but those days have passed. Today's workers are stranded and out of work if they are unable to retrain for a new job, perhaps a new career. We must train each person, all those who are out of work, to create the work they themselves can do and train them to market themselves through the internet. People trained in the industrial era do not have the skills to transform themselves into producers. Each person can create their own work and market that work if they are shown how. That is where the Community Training Center comes in.

Eventually, in every neighborhood across America and then in every neighborhood and village around the world, a Community Training Center will provide the education, training and resources required for each person to be self-sufficient in work. Everyone has a rationale for living, everyone was born with a purpose, everyone has a unique gift that they alone are qualified to present to the world. It is my firm belief that 90% of all people can become financially independent by offering their gift to the world. This will require training in identifying their gift, acquiring the skills to produce and monetize that gift and identifying the resources necessary to successfully market and deliver that product to eager customers. For those people who are unable to monetize their gift or for those whose monetization of their gift provides an inadequate income, additional training will be required in a field that provides the income they need. In such cases, each person will still be the architect of their own fate, but their primary gift will not be the vehicle which provides for their monetary needs.

Of course, there will be many people for whom self-employment will remain an alien and incomprehensible challenge. It will be an obstacle they cannot overcome. Hopefully, this will be a minority of people; otherwise we will be resurrecting dead dinosaurs. Does anyone recall the movie "Jurassic Park?" We all know how that turned out. Many people will be challenged by the thought of self-employment, fearing it won't work for them, that they have no marketable skills or that they are unable or unwilling to learn a new skill set. Generally speaking, people are going to have to get with the program or they will be left behind; tough love rules.

Fortunately, the Community Training Centers won't be teaching people to do something they do not want to do. The objective of the Community Training Center is to identify a person's unique skill, hidden talent or buried dream and then bring that to light. Next will be to train that person in the proper employment of that skill. Failure is not an option, neither is quitting and the Community Training Center possesses the technology to ensure that the vast majority of students will be successful. The principles of success have been discovered, so have the principles of failure. After over 20 years of research I have determined that failure is not the result of inadequate planning, inadequate capital, inadequate education, inadequate business acumen, inadequate marketing, inadequate commitment or inadequate work. To paraphrase Henry

Ford "whether you think you can or you can't, you're
right." Napoleon Hill identified the same principle; it's not
what you do that determines success, it's what you think. In
other words, it's a belief state. Tony Robbins has shown
that although beliefs may be near impossible to change,
under the right conditions and with the proper motivation
and encouragement, any belief can be changed. The door to
success does not swing open with action, it swings open
with thought. Once the door is open, then anyone can walk
through; only then you can take the action required to bring
your dreams to light. If the door remains closed, it doesn't
matter how much action you take, you can't get through a
closed door.

Poverty

Poverty is a disease. It is similar to any other
disease such as alcoholism, obesity, addictions or even
cancer. Poverty is also a disease that is passed on from
generation to generation. A person raised in an affluent
home will tend to live an affluent lifestyle for the rest of
their life. A person who is raised in poverty will tend to
remain impoverished for the rest of their life. Take away all
the wealth and resources of a person raised in affluence and
in a few years they will most likely have regained all their
wealth. Give a large sum of money to someone raised in
poverty and they will tend to lose or spend all that money
within a few years with nothing to show for it. Affluence as
well as poverty almost seem hereditary. Fortunately, there
are several very dramatic exceptions to the rule that those

raised in poverty remain in poverty; Oprah, Ted Turner, Richard Branson, Eminem, Jordin Sparks. Although these examples may seem to be the exception, they actually prove the thesis: whatever a person believes is what they will be. Community Training Centers are oriented on this principle; it is a person's belief that determines their fate and that belief can be modified. By establishing Community Training Centers in impoverished neighborhoods, the cycle of poverty and the cycle of violence caused by that poverty can be broken. We can win the war on poverty using the technology of today. Community Training Centers will do it. I am not asking you to believe me, I am asking you to accept the results whatever they may be. If the Community Training Center program proves successful, it should be rolled out as quickly as possible across the nation, if it should fail, we must allow it to fail and then set about creating a new system that works. I don't believe in excuses, I believe in results.

Corporations in The New Economy

Corporations big and small will continue to play a role in the new economy. But the concept of the corporation must change to match the realities of the new era.

Corporations must be more responsive to their customers. Each corporation must produce the best quality and safest products possible. Employees must have a say in management of the corporation. Restructuring the corporation to produce safe, quality products requires an educated and experienced workforce organized into efficient teams using the best possible practices with the best raw materials. Most corporations already know how to do this, although there are many which do not take advantage of this knowledge. The market must decide which corporations will thrive and which will die. All managers and all those aspiring to be managers should be certified by completing a specified course of training and education in management methods. This should not be a legal requirement but should be an option that corporations may want to consider.

Corporate officers, managers and employee leaders should attend management skill training, training in productivity, supply chain and operational efficiency and other such training as is appropriate for their duties and career track. Seminars and workshops may be provided in-house or by organizations established for such purpose. Many of these types of organizations exist today.

Made In The USA must be something we are proud of. Whatever item holds that label must be of the highest quality at the best possible price. We must be proud of our goods, we must be proud of those who make them and we must be proud of those who steer those organizations in which those goods are made. There can be no more ponzi schemes. No more bribes, corruption or nepotism. No more greed. No more lust for power. No more Enron's, no more Lehman Brothers, no more bank bailouts. The American people are sick and tired of the big corporations and their corruption, greed, favoritism by Congress and nepotism. All this must stop. We cannot legislate morality, but we can adopt legislation that changes the function and role of the corporation to meet the realities of today.

As the economy and the world we live in is restructuring, so we must also restructure the corporation:

10% of all profits must be distributed to employees.

10% of all profits must be returned to the community from which they are derived as a direct check or direct deposit to each resident.

10% of all profits must be set aside for charity or to community non-profit organizations. This may be churches, schools, student tuition, college scholarships, medical or dental clinics, community health or dental insurance for those who can't afford it, heating oil assistance, food banks, animal shelters, the local Y, health club memberships, Boy's or Girl's Clubs, snow removal fund, infrastructure development or library funding. If a community has a need, the corporation has the option of addressing that need, but cannot forsake its commitment to the community in some way.

10% of all issued stock must be distributed to employees. This may be preferred stock if so desired by the corporation. If the corporation pays dividends, the holders of the stock must receive the dividends which are properly due. This stock may be held in a trust established by the corporation with the employees as beneficiaries or the stock may be distributed directly to each employee.

10% of the members of the Board of Directors (but no less than one), must be randomly chosen employees who shall represent all employees and communicate proceedings to employees. These members shall serve one year terms and serve in addition to their normal work activities. Any employee may opt out of Board membership.

Natural Resources

Natural resources, whether that be water, timber, coal, oil or gas, et al, belong to the community in which they are located. The community may license the harvest of these resources to any entity for a reasonable and appropriate license fee. This fee may be an annual fee or based on each unit of resource extracted. The community has the option to decide whether this fee shall be distributed to each resident directly by check or provided to a community fund established for that purpose.

Offshore natural resources within 200 miles of the coast belong to the nation. The appropriate federal agency will issue the necessary license(s) for the harvest of said resources. The license will include a per unit fee assessed to the holder of the license. The federal agency will collect and aggregate all fees and distribute 85% of all fees in the following month in the form of a check or direct deposit to each resident and citizen of the United States age 13 and older. 15% of the fees received will be retained by the agency for administrative costs.

From the ages of 13 to 18, these receipts will be retained in a family trust managed by the head of household or designee thereof. The beneficiaries will be each member of the family from age 13 to 18. These funds cannot be spent but they may be invested in authorized secure investment instruments. These instruments may include local, community or municipal bonds. Funds may also be held by a local or community bank, savings and loan or credit union. National banks or investment firms shall not hold these trust funds. Funds will be released to each beneficiary upon reaching age 18 in a manner determined by the trust agreement.

Cable TV

The cables carrying cable services are a community resource. The community owns the cable line and must pay for the installation and maintenance of said cable lines.

No community has the authority to issue a monopoly license to any cable service provider. Making the cable lines a public resource allows for any cable provider to provide cable service to any household. Each household may have a different cable service provider. Open competition will assure competitive market prices for cable service. The community may decide whether or not to tax any cable service provider for the use of the community's cable lines.

A QUICK LESSON IN ECONOMICS

A quick lesson in economics: Let's say you are at an auction. Perhaps there are as many as 100 other people there also. This auction features rare paintings, unique artwork and period pieces. All of it is very fashionable and very valuable. But this auction has a couple of unique rules.

1. You only have 25 dollars to bid with.
2. You can only use that 25 dollars to bid. You cannot use your own outside money or other people's money.
3. You may not group with anyone else to form a bidding club or pool.

The first piece comes out. The curator describes the piece and the artist and how meticulously and lovingly the artist has worked on this one piece over the last 2 years. The auctioneer then begins the auction. People look at each other as the bidding begins. The auctioneer starts the auction at 5 dollars. After all, everyone knows that each person in the room only has 25 dollars with which to bid and it is believed that many people may want to acquire more than one piece of art.

A hand goes up. The bid is 5 dollars. A nod from a gentleman in the corner raises the bid to 7.50. A matron raises the bid to 10 dollars. The auctioneer continues his spiel but there are no further bids. The delicate piece of art is sold to the woman for 10 dollars.

Another piece of art is presented. Again this astonishing, valuable piece is described in complete detail. It is considered highly valuable; one of the most highly valued pieces at this auction. Again the bidding begins; 5 dollars, 6 dollars, 7 dollars, 10. The bid finally rests at 12 dollars, nearly half of what any one person can spend in the room.

The next piece, a rare commodity, is presented. The auction begins at 7 dollars and quickly increases to 15 dollars. At this point it slows to a crawl but continues its upward climb. At 20 dollars there is another bidding war and the price finally reaches the maximum of 25 dollars. A very pleased young man has won the auction. Being the sole bidder at the maximum allotment, he is very pleased to be able to take this distinguished item of artwork home.

The lesson to be learned here is that no one individual can bid anymore than 25 dollars. No piece of artwork, regardless of its estimated value can be worth any more than 25 dollars because that's the maximum that can be spent on any one piece.

This is what happens in a zero inflation economy. The prices of commodities and goods remain connected to the price of the currency. Only extraordinary events in supply or demand or outside factors can influence the price of the artwork in the room. Of course, a zero inflation economy is impractical in a modern world of fluctuating supply and demand from one market to another, but price hikes and shortages would not be dependent upon the value of the currency, they would solely be dependent on factors Other than the value of the currency.

Now let's say a wealthy gentleman enters the room. He gives each person in the room an additional 25 dollars. The rules are adjusted permitting each person to bid up to 50 dollars. And so they do. The auction continues but the prices of artwork sold have increased. Does this mean the artwork has increased in value? Did the inherent worth of the art suddenly jump? No, the artwork is still made of the same material. The same artists still created their beautiful pieces. The time involved in creating each piece has not changed. The only thing that has changed is the amount of money in the room. More money equals inflation; nothing else can affect inflation. Only the money supply in the marketplace establishes the rate of inflation.

We are back at the auction. This time, instead of entering the room the wealthy gentleman stands just outside of it. Each person in the room has their 25 dollars but each hour they are given another dollar. Not only that, but the wealthy gentleman outside of the room has declared that whatever the price of a piece may rise to, within "reasonable" limits, he will guarantee that the winning bidder can borrow the money to cover the difference.

What happens now? The auctioneer, the auction house owner and the curator meet for a hurried conference. They understand that each person in the room will receive 1 dollar for each hour that passes. They decide to introduce several breaks to extend the duration of the auction. This alone will put more money in their pocket. The auctioneer, auction house owner and curator also decide upon an additional strategy: Over time, they can raise the initial bid on each piece - within "reasonable limits." After all, the wealthy gentleman - an uncle of several people in the room - has guaranteed to loan the money for a winning bidder to purchase a piece they really like by allowing them to borrow the money. The auctioneer, the auction house owner and the curator all resume their positions. The auction house owner stands at the back of the room, a big smile on his face. He knows this can only end in his favor as he sneaks a glance at the rich uncle beside him. After all, the rich uncle has guaranteed to lend enough money to pay for any artwork purchased by a winning bidder. The auction begins anew.

What can we expect to happen? Several things will happen including one we may not have anticipated. First, the first piece of art does indeed begin at a higher bid, 7 dollars rather than the customary 5 dollars for a rather ordinary piece. The people in the room, not entirely certain of how this process will play out bid warily. This piece goes to 20 dollars, a little high perhaps but still within the range of the maximum it could have been. The next piece is also introduced at 7 dollars. Bidding goes a little higher with each piece until the magic 25 dollar limit is passed. The next bidder bids 27 dollars and glances at his uncle who nods his head, his bid will be covered, acknowledging this he wins the bid. The auction continues.

The auction moves forward and more and more people bid on each piece. More and more people become accustomed to the process; the old way of bidding is becoming a forgotten memory. The auction seems to be taking on an almost game like atmosphere. With the guarantee of the rich uncle at the back of the room, bidders feel encouraged to bid the price of the art higher and higher. Because the rich uncle has guaranteed their bid, the bidders bid more and more with some even bidding more than their 25 dollars and borrowing 25 dollars or more from their uncle. The auctioneer, the auction house owner and the curator are of course, quite pleased because each of them will receive a portion of the profits.

As the auction continues, the auctioneer begins each bid at a slightly higher bid than the previous bid - at a price he feels is "reasonable." If the rich uncle at the back of the room indicates the bid is unreasonable, the auctioneer lowers the bid until the wealthy uncle agrees that the bid is reasonable. This newer "reasonable" starting point is always, of course, a bit higher than the previous initial bidding price.

What we see is this: with the rich uncle guaranteeing the price of each purchased artwork, it is inevitable that the price of the artwork will rise over time. Another event we may not have expected is that some people bid everything they have, knowing that anything they "really" need or want will be covered by the rich uncle. They are discouraged from saving money because they know their rich uncle will cover their needs, and they are encouraged to spend money freely to generate a higher standard of living. They are also encouraged to borrow money freely to increase their "income." But their income is not actually increasing, it is in fact declining, because their money buys less and less at a rate which cannot keep pace with the increases.

Others not only bid everything they have, they also borrow heavily from the rich uncle simply to achieve more expensive artwork. With this more expensive artwork, the winning bidders can now proudly display it, proving to themselves and their neighbors not only how important and special they are, but also how successful they are at the "game."

An unintended consequence and perhaps one that will escape our attention is this: because the rich uncle has lent money to the winning bidders, the winning bidders have used the artwork they have won as collateral for the loan the uncle provided them. In essence, the uncle now owns nearly all the artwork in the room. All the assets have transferred to the rich uncle while much of the cash has transferred to the auctioneer, the auction house owner and the curator. The winning bidders are essentially left only with loan notes which they must pay back to their uncle. The winning bidders can enjoy their fine artwork, they may display their artwork proudly, but they are all living on borrowed time because the rich uncle is the true owner of the artwork and may call in the loan at any time.

To complicate things further what if the auctioneer, the auction house owner and the curator are all working in conjunction with the rich uncle? Wouldn't these four then split all the cash and all the assets between them leaving the bidders with worthless pieces of paper? Now what would happen if at some point - after the majority of bidders find themselves indebted to the uncle but still borrowing heavily - the rich uncle suddenly stops supplying the bidders with more money? The auction probably won't stop as a few dollars are most likely still in possession of many people in the room, but the affect would be to cause a large downturn in the process. Prices may drop, more and more people would find themselves "inactive", unable to participate in the auction because the weight of their debts is too heavy and the income they were receiving was only borrowed money from their uncle. In order to raise cash, the bidders can sell their few pieces of artwork to the auction house. This then transfers some of the artwork back to the auction house where the auction house can hold it or sell it again at auction as they see fit. After a time, the uncle begins loaning money again and the process begins once more. With the auction house and the uncle working together, these "boom and bust" cycles can be initiated at regular intervals calculated to move the most amount of assets and cash to both the rich uncle and the auction house partners.

Does this sound anything like our economy today? Doesn't this represent what is going on with rising costs in health care? Is this the cause of rising costs in higher education? If the government stopped loaning many to schools and hospitals, for healthcare and tuition, we may experience a difficult period in which we need to relearn the rules of personal finance and the principles of a new economy, but in the long term, it would be much better for us as a people.

A CREDIT ECONOMY

The economy of the United States and of the world is based on a debt economy. This concept is a relatively new phenomenon. This concept of an economy was introduced to the United States with the advent of the income tax and the Federal Reserve. In Europe, a de facto economy of this nature had been in operation for many years. Established, organized and administered by the House of Rothschild, the debt economy reversed the traditional view of money from that of a credit currency – based on hard assets, often gold or land and capital creation – to that of a debt currency and capital depletion. From 1916 to 1971, this economy slowly transferred the wealth of the nation and of individual citizens into the hands of the bankers. In 1971, President Nixon moved the United States off the gold standard. This act decoupled the dollar from its hard asset backing which provided the stability and strength of the dollar. As a result, the transfer of wealth from the nation and its citizens into the Federal Reserve and the bankers accelerated at an ever increasing pace. Our free floating fiat currency began to decline in value and today stands at just 5% of the value from that of the dollar at the turn of the last century.

The view of the market that the generations raised under the auspices of the debt economy was – and is – that of a consumerism, hedonistic, materialistic, instant gratification perspective. People expect their needs and desires to be instantly fulfilled, the toys and bling they seek can be bought on credit, and the lifestyle they adopt is based on appearances – we have a bigger house, nicer car and take better vacations than you. Often these baubles come at the expense of a second or third mortgage and crushing debt. People understand that in order to live the lifestyle they desire, they must go into debt to achieve it. Rather than putting money into savings, people use credit cards to maintain their lifestyles. For the affluent and upper middle class, the social norm is that to increase wealth, investments must be made in the stock market, mutual funds, speculative financial derivatives and high yield junk bonds. For most investors, all of these investments are funded by debt. These investments and the debt by which they are funded all serve to transfer the wealth of the investor into the accounts of the creditor. The common investor is not creating capital, rather their capital is depleting – and that was how it was intended.

Until the early 1900's, investors understood that capital appreciation was based on capital creation; the acquisition of hard assets which paid a periodic income and increased in value over time. Today's investors have taken the exact opposite approach. Their investments are based primarily on paper assets which can depreciate over time and often do not pay any income. The blame does not belong to the investor. The system was created to do just that. Since all of today's investors were born after the introduction of this type of economy, this approach to investing is the only form of investment they know. Yet, there are a few whose investment strategy is one of true capital creation. They are the creditors from whom we borrow the money to sustain and expand our lifestyles. We pledge to them our hard (and hard earned) assets in exchange for a paper promise. Not only have we mortgaged our assets, the paper we purchase is subject to the volatility of the stock market and the economy. It is not unusual for an investor to be wiped out overnight. A stock market crash can decimate the life savings – held in paper investments – of any investor.

Modern market cycles are often based on the introduction or the withdrawal of cash from the economy. When credit is plentiful and easy to get, the market booms. When money is hard to come by and credit is difficult if not impossible to obtain, the market crashes. These cycles are often intentional and created by Federal Reserve monetary policy. The Federal Reserve works in concert with international and central banks and therefore, a recession in one location often spreads around the world.

Todays truly wealthy are our creditors. They hold our mortgages and extend our credit. Their wealth is based on tangible income generating stable assets while our wealth is based on intangible, speculative assets which pay no income.

There are many who proclaim that a return to the gold standard will heal the evils of our economy, revitalize our markets and strengthen our dollar. This is unlikely. Part of the reason is that there are far too many dollars in circulation around the world. Another part of the reason is that there is not enough gold to back a multi-trillion dollar economy. Returning the dollar to the gold standard would only sustain our current recession. If enacted sometime in the future during a robust period, the economy would falter and possibly plunge into recession.

There is an alternative method to stabilize and strengthen the dollar which is suitable for a modern global economy. The stabilization and strengthening of the dollar would also revitalize our economy and get people back to work. The economy would once again begin to expand. To stabilize the dollar, the dollar should be indexed to the level of national productivity and of capital creation. Because inflation is caused by an overabundance of money entering the economy, the creation of new money must be held to the growth rate of productivity and capital creation. Because the rate of productivity can be measured and systemized and capital creation is a tangible asset, growth of the money supply affixed to these indices will hold inflation at or near zero. To achieve these goals requires that we decouple the dollar and our debt from the hands of the Federal Reserve and international bankers. Obviously they won't be happy about this and, with their control of the world media and the halls of power, we will face powerful opposition in implementing this plan. But it can be done and it must be done if we are to reclaim our wealth and create a prosperous society.

CONGRESS

The members of each House of Congress will be limited to two terms.

Pensions must be privatized. Pension rates must be assessed on a pro rata basis commensurate with prevailing corporate rates.

Health care must be privatized.

No member of either House may accept a gift of any kind. Any gift so received shall not be declined, but must be forwarded within 90 days to the Smithsonian, Library of Congress or such other institute as designated by Congress.

Neither the House nor Senate may vote themselves an increase in pay. Increase in compensation will occur automatically each year commensurate with the increase in median middle class income.

Any law passed by Congress will apply as equally to Congress and the Federal Government as it does to the constituency to whom it is addressed. All past legislation from which Congress has exempted itself shall now apply to Congress.

All professional lobbying is prohibited. Citizens and citizens alone must be able to travel to D.C. to meet with their respective Congressman or Senator and voice their concerns. Special interests and professional lobbyists must not drown out the voice of American citizens.

One half of the Senate and one third of the House will be selected by random lot from the residents of their respective districts or states. Each citizen so selected will serve for one term. A citizen so chosen may decline their selection. Should the initial citizen so chosen decline their appointment, the next available alternate will be asked to accept the appointment. Should the second choice also decline, the lot will fall to a pool of volunteers established for that purpose. A member of this pool will be chosen at random and the pool will be renewed annually.

The House will originate all bills. Bills shall be introduced by a Congressman on their own, on behalf of a Senator or on behalf of a citizen of their district. Corporations, non-profit organizations, state legislatures or officials, communities or citizen groups may request their Representative submit a bill on their behalf. Each Congressman may decide whether or not to introduce to the House any bill request they receive. Rules regarding passage of a bill by the House shall be determined by members of the House. Each bill passed by the House shall move to the Senate for review and final passage into law.

The object of the Senate will be to prevent a bill from passing into law and to review current law to dismiss existing legislation. Committees of the Senate shall review each bill and existing law for environmental impact, community impact, commercial impact, legal impact, Constitutional compliance, impact on foreign policy and obligations and international treaties and trade agreements and any and all other such areas as the Senate may so determine. Members of the Senate shall determine what degree of negative impact is necessary to prevent a bill from passage or to dismiss an existing law.

No professional lobbying of the Senate or of Senators is permitted at any time while a member remains a member of the Senate.

Congressional Funding

Corporations may provide funds to any political candidate they choose up to the limits of said funding as provided by law. These limits may be raised upon implementation of the following: Each House of Congress shall establish a Funding Trust. Corporations must deposit all funding into this trust. Trust executors will then disperse the funds received for a candidate or current member in the amount received for that member but shall hold the donor anonymous. Political parties, action committees, campaign committees and citizen groups may donate directly to the candidate or member of their choice up to limits as established by law.

EDUCATION

We all know there are good teachers and bad teachers. We all know there are good schools and bad schools, good neighborhoods and bad neighborhoods. We all know there are good educational methods and bad methodologies. We all know there are good administrators and bad administrators. We all know there are good school committee members and bad committee members. The question is not whether there is good or bad, the question is; what do we do about it?

Bad teachers must be fired. Bad schools must be closed or transformed. Bad communities must be upgraded.

Principals must have the authority to dismiss teachers as they deem necessary. School committees must have the authority to review school curricula and the performance of teachers and school officials. Parents must have a say in what their children are being taught and in how the school operates and functions. Students must also have a voice in the operation of their school and in identifying inept teachers and officials.

Students must have exposure to athletics, art and music.

All this is only the beginning to upgrading our schools and educating our students to the standards established by the best schools in the world. In most measures of education, American students rank poorly, often not even in the top 20 of major nations. Proper education is a necessity for the United States to regain its predominance in the world. Without students moving into the workforce or on to college with the best possible education in the world, the United States will continue to lose respect among nations, our standard of living will continue to decline, crime and teenage pregnancy will increase and our industrial and commercial bases will continue to erode. Without the highest standards in education, the high caliber of recruit necessary for a modern and professional military will dwindle eroding the effectiveness and capability of our armed forces.

We cannot regain our position as best nation in the world by having the worst student education in the world. Our students deserve better and our nation needs better. American students must have at least a commensurate level of education with the best nations in the world.

The secondary educational system of the United States is broken and we know it. Many of us also know how to fix it but are prevented from doing so by Teacher's Unions, incumbency, tenure policy, resistance to change within a school or community or by politicking. In all cases, it is the children who suffer. The current educational system seems to have been adopted by J.P. Morgan and others late in the 19th century and early in the 20th century who sought a factory-type system to create drones and subservient individuals for their factories and wars. In contrast, the one room school house – although archaic and antiquated to us today – worked. Students of all ages assembled into one room. The teacher taught the students and created a lesson plan – for each student. Each student progressed throughout their school age years at their own pace. The teacher monitored their progress and guided students to the next level of their studies. We think of it as an overly simplistic system, but it worked, it produced results we are unable to duplicate today.

Alexis de Tocqueville, in his tour of America in the mid 1800's, stated that in each home he visited, he found at least two books: One was the Bible, the other was a copy of Shakespeare. Our 19th century students, regardless of whether they left school as early as 12 or 13, were well-educated, knowledgeable in mathematics and English grammar, they knew and understood world history and world geography, they were familiar with business, economics and politics – and they were well-read. The one room schoolhouse seems so primitive to us today, but its results were anything but primitive. Today's world requires different emphasis on learning, different skill sets and knowledge, but the results we seek must be at least comparable to world standards – and the one room schoolhouse of yesteryear.

The United States must establish a realistic system which provides for an individual's growth in reasoning ability, creativity, problem solving, financial education, systems knowledge, social interaction, team work, building teams, leadership, physical activity, community activityand vision. Each student must also learn financial discipline, including entrepreneurship from the earliest stage and will be introduced to passive income vehicles and other financial tools and measures. The goal of the financial curriculum is for each student to become financially independent upon graduation from secondary school. I believe these goals are achievable.

Our public secondary schools must become the best in the world and teams will be formed to travel to each country or location with a world-class middle or secondary school to observe its policies, methods, techniques and educators and provide recommendations to the President. The Department of Education will be retained only upon its conversion to the assembling, training and sending of these international teams and to assembling, training and sending teams of citizens throughout the nation to each middle and secondary school and community thereof and work with them to convert their school into a world-class, high performing, fun institution of middle or secondary education.

Throwing money at a problem does not fix the problem. Often the sudden influx of money only exacerbates the problem and/or contributes to cronyism, corruption and greed. We must invest in our students using methods that produce positive results. That does not necessarily mean we have to spend more money. Although the nations of Europe have invested heavily in their children's education by heavy taxation, I believe we can achieve the same results without excessive – or any aditional – taxation. What we need is a reorientation of our educational methodologies, not the inundation of our schools with cash that would, if no effective plan was established for its use, only be wasted and misused. The schools of our European allies have produced results that we here in the U.S. can only – now – envy, but we can find a way to achieve those results without extensive outlays of cash.

College and Universities

American colleges and universities are the best in the world; we must keep them that way. To assure this, we must leave the colleges and universities alone, we cannot impose government regulations, rules or guidelines. Colleges and universities work best when government stays out of their way.

The mandate of our colleges and universities is to produce a well-rounded individual with an understanding of global affairs. They are not training grounds for corporate drones, (regardless of the trend in that direction). Neither do colleges or universities educate students in the fundamentals of financial discipline – that has not been their mandate. An education in financial discipline will educate a student to achieve financial independence in the shortest time possible utilizing the best investment vehicles available. That type of education is taught in very few – if any – college or university, but it is part of the core curriculum at Community Training Centers.

The American college and university experience is a fundamental requirement in a global market. You can get by without such an experience, but if you have a choice to attend a college or university or not, go to school. The college and university experience is about new adventures, new explorations and new education within the relative safety of a community of like-minded peers.

The college and university experience is about achieving academic goals, expanding your mind, understanding alternative points of view, hard work and discipline. It is also about meeting others your own age from places you may never visit or, perhaps, never even knew existed. This experience exposes you to new points of view, new trains of thought, new streams of consciousness and new independence – no more mommy or daddy telling you when to get up or do your homework. You build relationships with others from around the world – or around the state, you get the opportunity to travel to exotic locations during spring break, attend concerts, roll through the nightclubs and bars, get introduced to new bands and great music, experience great sex and ridiculous parties. The college experience in America is supposed to be fun; don't get drowned in the tedium of hard work and study when there is so much fun to be had.

I see no reason that, with the proper discipline and planning, you can't get a 4.0 while partying your a$* off. It may take you an additional year, but you can do it.

The last two years of a four year institute has traditionally been devoted to career and vocational training and education. But we also need students with a well rounded perspective and an awareness of global affairs. America cannot compete without students knowledgeable about the plight of villagers in Africa, female circumcision, the spread of AIDS and famine in Third World countries, the viewpoint of women in Saudi Arabia and of young people in China. The world is shrinking. The globe is now a local place. The world is now our community. We must know our community, understand our community, protect our community and nurture our community. We may not always agree, but we do not need to resort to violence, we may not understand each other but we need not throw racial and ethnic slurs, we may not see eye to eye, but that doesn': mean we can't work shoulder to shoulder. All this is part of the mandate of the American college and university; to understand the world we live in, develop a greater awareness of the customs and cultures of people around the world and seek ways to cooperate to create a better world for all. This is what it means to attend college in America.

The Brain Drain

American colleges and universities are considered the best in the world by multiple international standards. We may not be aware of this here in the U.S. but the rest of the world is acutely aware of this. As a result, students from over a hundred countries around the globe attend a college or university somewhere in the United States each year. These students are often the best and the brightest within their respective communities. And each year, within weeks of receiving their degree, we send them home when their greatest desire is to remain.

These students have been away from home for four years; they have made friends, worked hard, spent countless hours in study and planted roots in the community. Many would prefer to remain in the States and raise a family here. Some want to start a business. But we don't allow them that option. Instead, we send the best and brightest the world has to offer away to rival corporations, competitive countries and competing markets. This is a great tragedy and mistake. When we could have the best, brightest and most well educated students in the world living here creating new inventions, building new businesses, developing alternative sources of energy, raising families and integrating into the social fabric of our nation, we choose instead to send them away. It is redundant to mention what they will do when they reach home. We are frittering away our opportunity. We are helping friends, allies and rivals to compete against us, instead of retaining this superior talent and developing the engines of tomorrow with the students of today. We must put an end to this brain drain:

Matriculating students from any post secondary school must be allowed to remain here in the US, without further visa or immigration requirements if they choose to do so. This is a simple and practical solution. We have no time to waste in implementing it.

POLICE REFORM

As there are good teachers and bad teachers, there are also good cops and "bad" cops. Although the vast majority of police officers have only the best interests of the community at heart and their actions reflect such disposition, there exists a small minority of police officers who feel they are above the law, maintain an attitude of arrogance or racism, believe physical force and violence is permissible against citizens and generally present an example of the worst that a police officer can be. These officers reflect poorly on a noble and dangerous profession and only serve to spread distrust and apprehension within the community. Officers of this nature must be stopped and held accountable for their actions. The following two measures should go far in remedying this situation.

A. Citizens Police Defense Task Force – A volunteer group of community members will monitor all police communications on a 24/7 basis. Upon each and every encounter between a police officer and a civilian, an on-call volunteer will be dispatched to the location of the interaction. This volunteer will remain at least 30 feet from the police officer and shall video the encounter from said distance seeking to provide the best vantage point to film the entire interaction as thoroughly and clearly as possible. Audio must also be recorded. Whenever possible, the interaction will be live-streamed to a community, regional or national website established for such purpose. The encounter will be recorded and archived for future review and evidence as necessary in a place immune to all police and federal search and seizure.

B. Citizens Police Review Committee –
   a. Pool of community volunteers. Any and all adult members of the community are eligible.
   b. 5 members will be selected at random from the pool for each review action.
   c. No member may serve sequentially (on more than one case back to back) unless not enough volunteers are available.
   d. Review every allegation of police brutality, mistreatment or excessive force.
   e. Hear testimony from all parties.
   f. Receive and review evidence.
   g. Assess evidence and testimony and produce a finding.
   h. The finding shall either dismiss the allegation or recommend the allegation for prosecution to the appropriate authority.
   i. The finding will specify the allegation, note the evidence and testimony, identify all participants and officers, modify the

resultant allegation as necessary to suit the evidence and testimony, dismiss any portion of the allegation against any officer and/or recommend specific action to be taken against officers deemed responsible for the allegation to wit; fine, suspension, termination, incarceration, education or training and public and written apology to victim, family and community and if so determined, forwarding the finding to the proper legal authority for prosecution.

j. Upon submission of the finding to prosecution, the head of the Police Department shall suspend all officers named in the finding as responsible within 14 days of submission of the finding.

k. The Committee will forward copies of all results regardless of the nature of the finding, to local or regional media, internet media or sites, head of the Police Department and to the appropriate legal authority if necessary and to the appropriate municipal administrative official, (Mayor, town council, etc).

l. The Committee shall archive a copy of all findings as established by procedure.

SOCIAL SECURITY

Social Security is the elephant in the room no one talks about, it is also the 800 pound gorilla that is eating everything in our kitchen. Along with Medicare and Medicaid, Social Security consumes the largest portion of the federal budget. This cost to the federal government must be reduced while retaining the level of benefits due to current and future generations.

a.   The stock market is a varying market that has no place in providing assurance for future generations.

b.   A 40 year plan should be adopted. Those just entering the work force and those with over 39 years remaining to retirement should have their funds dedicated to other sources. Those who have less than one year to retirement will have no change to their apportionment or benefits. Between 40 years and 1 year a slope of funding apportionment should be adopted. Wealth is generated not from the stock market but by investing in profitable investments. An investment must pay dividends – whether in the form of dividends, royalties, license or patent fees, copyright fees, rents or income from income trusts. The funds being contributed to the Social Security trust fund should be invested in these investments which pay a profit, interest or dividends from day one. The investments sought for inclusion with the fund are those which have historically provided the greatest return and which are expected to continue that trend.

This new fund will pool all monies received and invest said receipts in annuities, bonds, preferred stock, royalties, license fees, copyrights, music publishing rights, REITs, MLPs, BDCs, ETFs, secure oil and gas income trusts, natural resource rights, TIPS, Treasury bills, notes and bonds, asset backed securities, unit investment trusts, patent rights, factoring, private lending, transactional real estate funding, asset leasing and tax liens and notes, et al. I expect the growth rate of this fund to be at least equivalent to the rate of inflation and could reach as high as an annual 10% to 12% or more.

For those entering the workforce and for those with 40 years or more remaining until retirement, 100% of their Social Security contribution will be deposited into the new fund. For those with less than one year until retirement, there will be no change in their benefits or the allocation of their contribution. The algorithm for determining the apportionment of an individual's Social Security contribution which will flow to the new fund is as follows:

2.5 times the number of years until their anticipated retirement

Example: Michael has been in the workforce for 10 years working full time for each week of those 10 years. Michael expects to retire in another 30 years. This year, and for each year until retirement, 75% of Michael's Social Security contribution will remit to the new fund. (30 x 2.5)

Julie has been working for 33 years. She is looking forward to her retirement in just 7 years. From this date until her retirement, 17.5% of Julie's annual Social Security contribution will remit toward the new fund.

Jay and his new bride Martha have just married, each has been working full time for just 2 years. Prior to this period, Jay and Martha were in college working part-time. Their level of income during that period was not high enough to trigger Social Security participation. Both Jay and Martha anticipate working full time (barring children), for at least the next 38 years. Jay hopes to work for at least 42 and possibly 45 or more years. Even though Jay may work for more than 38 years, this algorithm is based on a 40 year implementation period, therefore both Jay and Martha use 38 years as the basis to determine the amount of their Social Security contribution which will remit toward the new fund. As a result, from this year forward, 95% of Jay and Martha's Social Security contribution will remit toward the new fund.

David expects to retire in just two more years. Although David isn't certain how he will keep himself busy, he is looking forward to his retirement and is dreaming of traveling the country with his wife in their new RV, playing golf on golf courses around the country and spending the winters in a warm location, maybe Florida, Arizona or California. Because David has just two more years until retirement, 5% of David's annual Social Security contribution for each of the next two years will remit toward the new fund, (2.5 x 2).

Of course it is impossible to predict just how much the return will be for this new fund. I fully expect the ROI to outperform most standards of investment, but as they say in mutual funds, "past performance is no guarantee of future results."

I believe that this proposal is an essentially safe method to move Social Security into a private type system while retaining, if not increasing, the level of benefits projected to be provided by the current method. By utilizing only secure income instruments, this plan is safe and the level of return should exceed that which the current system provides while circumventing the volatility of the stock market.

IMMIGRATION

To say we have a problem with immigration is an understatement. Millions of immigrants currently reside within our borders, many of them illegal immigrants. Illegal immigration is illegal. However, to deport illegal immigrants at this stage in our nation's history will produce a trauma from which this nation may never heal. The reverberations and the eventual scar of any such deportation will resonate across the world and may cause strains in our foreign policy, produce stress in our international agreements, cause our friends and allies to rethink their position with us and may affect the influx of qualified students to our colleges and universities. A deportation of this nature will produce effects this nation cannot tolerate and it could affect our commercial dealings and adversely influence our trade partners around the world.

I feel the following measures are the best solution for this nation in addressing the immigration problem without creating more problems than it cures.

1. Blanket Amnesty – Any and all illegal immigrants currently residing within the US shall not be deported but will be assured of amnesty against deportation provided they obtain full identification documentation and a complete background check within 6 months.

Any immigrant participating in this program will receive an interim resident visa permitting them to reside within the country for two years under the condition they learn to speak passable English and know a high school level of geography, history and politics of the United States. After two years, each immigrant must present at a designated location and profess their English fluency and their knowledge of US geography, history and politics. Should they fail this assessment, they will be deported immediately without recourse and must meet all admittance requirements for future immigration.

2. Open Immigration – There will be no quotas for any country, race or ethnic group. However, prior to receiving a visa for admittance to the US, all applicants must speak passable English and prove their knowledge of American history, geography, economics, business, politics and religions. If accepted, and if the applicant seeks permanent residency or possible naturalization, they must pass a comprehensive background check (the results will not be held against them except for in case of capital crimes), and they will be issued a United States photo ID. This ID will be acceptable in all states and territories of the United States as proof of identification and must be on their person at all times when in public and must be relinquished for review by a government official or police officer whenever so requested.

3. Full Documentation – Application for a visa will require full documentation on the part of the applicant. This documentation shall include an acceptable birth certificate, life history outline and complete copies of all court and health records. Only evidence of commission of a capital crime will be grounds for denial of a visa. In the event no birth certificate is available, the United States Embassy or Consular Office will prepare an Immigration Birth Certificate using the best information possible for date and time of birth, location of birth and parentage.

4. Entrepreneurship/Self-Employment – In accordance with the new economy, each adult immigrant is expected to either start a new business within one year after entry to the US, or within 90 days begin training at a Community Training Center. Only upon failure of either a new business or self-employment and after a period of time as shall be determined, the immigrant will be eligible to seek a W2 job.

5. Legal Rights – As each immigrant is fully documented and has passed entry requirements to the United States, each immigrant shall be eligible for Social Security participation and any and all other benefits accorded to United States citizens and permanent residents after a period of 90 days. Any and all school age children may enroll in school immediately.

THE FEDERAL RESERVE

Prior to the establishment of the Federal Reserve, economic booms and busts seemed to cycle every twenty years or so. Since the establishment of the Federal Reserve, our economy bounces from boom to bust approximately every eight years. Prior to the Federal Reserve, our dollar was one of the strongest currencies in the world. Since the establishment of the Federal Reserve, the dollar has lost 95% of its value. Prior to the Federal Reserve, our economy was vibrant, dynamic, growing and strong. Since the establishment of the Federal Reserve, our economy has declined, our corporate competitiveness has eroded, millions of American jobs have transferred overseas, millions are out of work and the middle class is dropping into poverty levels. We can no longer afford the Federal Reserve. It must be terminated and its assets distributed appropriately as soon as possible. Debts owed to it by banks or government should be canceled.

The Federal Reserve is a semi-private, autonomous and anonymous organization. Behind the scenes, powerful bankers pull the strings. These strings stretch all the way into the halls of Congress, the corridors of the White House and, by extension, into the board rooms of corporations across the country. The influence of the Federal Reserve is felt by everyone; no one is immune to its whims or outside of its control. The Federal Reserve must be shut down as soon as possible.

The U.S. dollar is printed by the U.S. Mint. But that dollar is not the property of the U.S. government, it is the property of the Federal Reserve. The U.S. Mint incurs the expenses of printing and distributing the currency, the Federal Reserve does not. Once printed, each dollar is recorded on the books of the Federal Reserve and is then loaned back to the U.S. government with interest. The U.S. government prints the money, incurs the expense of doing so, hands the money it has printed to the Federal Reserve which then turns around and loans it to the U.S. government and the U.S. government must pay interest on the money it has printed while the Federal Reserve collects the profit. This is quite a good scam. Not only that but this grandest scam of all was written into law. Tell me there is not something wrong with this picture.

We need to disband the Federal Reserve, but first we must conduct a complete and comprehensive audit of its operations and assets. We need to know who has the money, what that money has bought, the type of assets the Federal Reserve holds and who is holding them. With this information in hand, we can then terminate the Federal Reserve and distribute its assets back to those from whom those assets were taken. After this audit, the dollars recorded on the books of the Federal Reserve shall return to the United States and all debt owed to the Federal Reserve canceled.

The ostensible purpose of the Federal Reserve was to regulate the currency and flatten out the fluctuations of a dynamic economy. The actual purpose was to control the currency, which it has done, create a debt economy, which it has done, transfer the wealth of the nation from the many to the few, which it has done and force the people to expect and depend on others and the federal government for their jobs, their health and their well being. All these things the Federal Reserve has accomplished. The innate power of the American people has been transferred to anonymous men in shadowy corridors, to megalithic federal agencies and departments, to big banks and big corporations. The time to retire the Federal Reserve is long overdue, it must be retired forthwith.

Gross Domestic Product

Gross Domestic Product – The GDP measures the wrong items. By measuring the mere exchange of goods and services we lose sight of the morals, ethics and humanity involved in each decision. There is no such thing as "it's not personal, it's just business", everything is personal when it's your job, your home, your paycheck or your family. We must initiate a dialogue that will create a real world index which measures a green world – educational status of our children and schools, volunteerism, preservation of farmlands, parks and natural areas, the number and degree of self sufficient communities and homes, innovation, entrepreneurship and new successful businesses. We must identify green paths to energy, dusting off old methods for new ideas, freeing the past to revitalize the future, issue patents and copyright on works and processes that work yet may operate beyond our simple understanding of today's science. The success of America's future depends on the foundations of the past, the institutions of today and the educational, entrepreneurial and innovative initiatives of the future. To stand idly by while other nations pass us in every conceivable measure is destructive and fool-hardy. The future is ours to take, but we must grasp it today. Should we fail to act, should we fail to grasp, should we fail to hold on tightly, the world will pass us by and America herself will fall becoming just so much more dust in the dustbin of history. We must measure the strength of our nation and its economy by three simple factors. It is these factors which measure true wealth. Happiness, love and peace are the factors by which we must measure our success as a people, as an economy and as a nation.

TAXATION AND THE IRS

There is no need for the IRS. The Internal Revenue Service is a giant, bloated, inhuman mechanism that can destroy lives, ruin businesses and tear families apart. If the IRS should accuse you of a tax crime, you are assumed to be guilty until you can prove your innocence. This is the opposite of the American way of justice. In America, you are always innocent until proven guilty by your accuser. This not true with the IRS.

The purpose of the IRS is to collect income taxes and enforce compliance with that collection. If you fail to pay your share of taxes, you can expect exorbitant penalties and possibly face jail time. We can do away with the IRS if we reduce the complexity of the tax system.

Part of reducing the level of complexity in taxation is to decrease taxation rates. Another part is to eliminate deductions. If we adopt a straight across the board 10% tax rate for individuals and 15% for corporations, the IRS and its complex code will not be necessary. We should also eliminate estate and capital gains taxes. If necessary, the United States may impose a 1% national sales tax in order to make up for any loss of revenue caused by the new tax rates. Taxes would remit directly to the U.S. Treasury Department. Instead of a huge IRS, a small streamlined Tax Office would be all that is necessary to record the amount if taxes received. We may wish to retain real estate deductions such as deductions on mortgage interest and real estate depreciation, but we should hold the line on any other deductions or tax credits.

DOMESTIC POLICY

We stand upon the threshold of tomorrow and we have a choice to make. We can choose destruction or we can choose life. That is the clearest and most realistic of all possibilities we face. There will be those who contend that this is wrong, that there is plenty of time, and that there are numerous choices. But that is a delusion. There may be many variations within our choice, but our primary choices remain the same, choose destruction or choose life. In choosing death, all we must do is nothing. We are a train hurtling along such a path today and we are nearly out of track. To choose life means to change everything. As Winston Churchill once said, there will be "blood, sweat and tears." We must shift from a consuming mentality to a prosuming mentality. We must shift from a debt economy to a savings economy. We must shift from instant gratification to delayed gratification. We must shift from a destructive ecology to a green ecology. To the greatest extent possible, each community and each home within that community must become self sufficient in its energy, food and water needs. Each car, aircraft and vehicle must be self-sufficient, self-sustaining and green in its energy use. Our office buildings, warehouses, factories, malls, hospitals and schools must all be self-sufficient in their energy needs. We must develop ways of seeing the future that are different from the ways we have traveled in the past. We must learn new ways of living which are comfortable and compatible with Earth and nature. If we continue to violate the laws of Spirit which govern physical reality, we will eventually reap the consequences such a choice assures.

Occupy Wall Street

At the time of this writing, October 2, 2011, students and others are demonstrating in the streets of America. From Wall Street in New York to State Street in Boston, the Financial District in Chicago and the offices of Bank of America in San Francisco, thousands are expressing their concerns and making their opinions known. At this point in time, these groups are disjointed, disorganized, without strong leaders and express no clear or central message. Yet, the general theme of these demonstrators is pervasive: Something is wrong with the system and the time has come to fix it. I support these demonstrations, and this Policy is, hopefully, a call to arms, not only for the demonstrators, but for all Americans and a declaration of a central message. The power of the federal government must be restored to the people, the big banks and big corporations must be reorganized and become more responsive to the public from whom they derive their profits and the capitalist system must be restructured to suit the needs, choices and realities of a civilization heading into greener pastures, greater information exchange and enhanced participation by all. This restructuring is occurring now and without conscience guidance and forethought, this process could run away from us and destroy the society from which it issues. We must grasp the reins of change and steer our society into safe harbor. Failure to direct this change to a fair and beneficial society will be to relinquish the potential of a better tomorrow to the madmen of yesterday. This cannot be allowed to happen.

What's Wrong with America?

We all know there is something wrong, we all know that things aren't right, we sense it in our bones, we feel it in our hearts, we see the destructive effects of this wrong every day. Friends and neighbors are out of work, maybe you are out of work. Millions of homes have been foreclosed. Thousands of homeless live on the streets, beneath bridges and in parks. Whole families fill our shelters. Millions of children go to bed each night with hungry bellies. Health care is unaffordable, necessary medicines are out of reach. Emergency rooms are overwhelmed by the influx of people with common ailments because they have nowhere they can go to obtain medical care. Meanwhile, trauma victims die on these same floors because the surgeons and nurses are overwhelmed. This is not a description of some third world nation. This is America – the United States of America. Obviously something is wrong, but what is it and how do we fix it?

In this book, I am presenting a series of answers and solutions I believe will work. I believe they will fix what is broken and right what is wrong. I don't have all the answers, I don't have all the solutions, and I am hoping you will help to provide the answers to the questions I am unable to answer. I am hoping you will present the solution to a problem I can't fix. I don't have all the answers, but I do know this – no answer or solution will last, if we as a nation do not return to our true root – to our one true foundation.

This nation was founded as a Christian nation. This country was settled by those seeking not so much a new way of life, but by those who sought the opportunity to worship God as they saw fit.

Separation of Church and State

"Congress shall make no law respecting an establishment of religion, or prohibiting the free exercise thereof…"

This clause in the First Amendment of our Constitution was, I believe, intended to prevent the establishment of a state religion as was common in Europe at the time of the writing of the Constitution. I believe it was not written to prevent Christian principles or the guidance of God from steering our nation. The goal of this clause was to permit people to worship God in the churches of their choice, in a manner they felt best, not to extinguish religion or decouple the people from God.

The problems of America are because we have lost our mooring, we have lost our way, we have lost our connection to God. Millions of those who do worship are Sunday Christians; God is a part of their life just one day a week, the rest of their life is devoted to the affairs of the world. Because the everyday American is no longer focused on God, and millions more do not acknowledge

God at all, we have lost our strength of purpose, our common vision and our moral foundation. The wisdom and insight needed to guide our nation effectively and lead our families strongly with vision and humility is a gift from God. Without a connection to God, we stumble and fall, we lose sight of goals, our families surrender to dysfunction and the path our nation treads becomes increasingly dark, immoral and fearful.

The secular community contends that morality is not a function of religion, not a gift of God, that it runs inherent within the human heart, and perhaps they are right, but the evidence seems otherwise. Gangs battle in our streets, drugs tear apart families and ruin lives, fathers disappear into the night forsaking their families, greed and power dominate our politics and drive our corporations. We have surrendered the best of what mankind can be to the fears, insecurities and depravity of the human heart. Without God we do not have the strength to overcome our worries, we do not have the wisdom or insight to lead our nation, corporations or families effectively, we do not have the will to do what is wrong when it is more expedient to do what is wrong. We have lost our way, we have lost our connection to God and we are paying the price of that loss.

We cannot legislate morality nor can we legislate religion. To return to our roots, to reestablish our firm foundation, to regain the vision and insight to lead our nation and lives into a bold, bright future, we must return to God. But this is not something we can write into law, it is not something we can require of our neighbors or demand of our children, it must be a free choice of each person, each individual, each child of God. It must be a decision we reach not collectively, but individually, it cannot be something we think with our mind, it must be something we feel in our heart. Each of us must make the first move to open our hearts to God, but it is God Himself who must make the next move to an open and willing people. God must send the Holy Spirit to this people, to every home in every city, into every boardroom and cubicle, into every office and hall of Congress. We must decide to submit our lives to God and only then can God send His Holy Spirit to begin the Great Revival this nation so desperately needs. I do not have all the answers, I do not even know all the questions, no one does, but God knows, God understands, God cares and God can lead.

The future of our nation depends on the decisions we make today. The families our children raise will be based on what we do now. God has made us certain promises; He has promised that if we yield our lives to Him and lead our nation with His guidance, He will man the watchtowers, guard the walls and take the field on our behalf. He will protect us from our enemies and deliver us from evil. He has promised that if we put Him first He will deliver prosperity and not poverty, He will bring hope and not fear, He will bring abundance and not famine, He will send us joys and not sorrows. We have a simple choice; we can continue to allow our nation its walk into the dark or we can change course and begin to walk toward the light.

Federal Audit

An audit of the military shall occur. Each major piece of military equipment shall be identified, numbered and accounted for. Each tank, truck, Humvee, ship, plane and helicopter shall be counted. Each soldier, sailor, airman and Marine shall be identified and accounted for. These figures will be presented to the President and appropriate authorities and may be provided to the American people. An audit of the Federal Reserve shall be undertaken and its results made public. An audit of all major banks in the United States shall be undertaken with special consideration given to those which received funds under TARP. The funds provided thereunto shall be identified as to disbursement and, if applicable, returned to the American people. Detailed results of this audit will be made public.

Federal Contracts

No future contract will be granted except through a competitive, public and open bid by those organizations presenting an acceptable response to a Request for Proposal. There will be no solo, noncompetitive or closed contracts granted.

The Patriot & Military Commissions Act

Both the Patriot Act and the later Military Commissions Act were knee-jerk reactions to a bad moment in American history. The events of 9/11 are a true tragedy, the lives of 3000 families were destroyed and this country will never be the same again. However, by passing laws that suspended the Constitution, depriving Americans of their rights, their right to due process and habeas corpus, these were the wrong response to a tragic event.

Both the Patriot Act and the Military Commissions Act should be dropped, at the very least they should be allowed to expire. There is no justification for violating the Constitution or of passing Presidential Directives that ignore the law.

The TSA

Whether or not we need the TSA is debatable; that we need some form of airport security is not. The TSA must find other means of screening passengers and identifying potential terrorists and others who would do harm to the passengers or aircraft in flight. Israel has one of the best – if not the best – security systems in place at its airports. The TSA and federal government have much to learn from a nation that has been fighting terrorists since the day of its birth in 1948.

The process the TSA currently uses to screen passengers is intrusive, inhumane and is a violation of the Constitution. A way must be found to bring the screening process in line with the law and due process.

Customs Roadblocks

U.S. Customs and other federal agencies have established mobile roadblocks in various parts of the country. These roadblocks stop each car and vehicle and ask the driver and passengers if they are Americans. This is insane. Any terrorist would simply reply "Yes" and be on his merry way. The purpose of these roadblocks seems designed not to catch terrorists and illegal aliens, but rather to intimidate ordinary Americans and get people used to the idea that, on any travel across the country, you must present your "papers" or be hauled off to prison. This tactic seems designed to scare Americans into blindly obeying the federal government and these so called checkpoints have no legitimate purpose. They should cease at once.

The FDA and Water Resources

The FDA and the big corporations control our food supply. It is now illegal to transport food you have grown across state lines. The FDA has raided Amish farms and organic growers for raising, transporting or selling unregistered food. The ostensible purpose is to prevent outbreaks of disease caused by tainted crops. It is possible that these crops may be tainted in some natural process or as the result of some domestic farming process, but the most likely source of food borne illness is the federal government. This seems to be just another tactic on the part of the federal government to control the people, to squash private initiative and quell dissent in any form; it seems more a measure of ensuring compliance with federal authorities and getting people to kowtow to federal authority. Americans don't need a license to grow their own food, nor is it illegal to do so, regardless of what any law may claim. The only entity that benefits from these laws is the big corporations; they are the only entity that has the resources to comply with all the regulations and supply food to the American population. Americans don't need another law stuffed down their throat especially when it benefits big corporations. This law and related laws and regulations need to be terminated.

Water

The U.S. Army Corps of Engineers controls all the fresh water in the nation. You think your favorite, secret hidden away fishing spot belongs to you? Guess again. You think the stream behind your farm is free for you to use? Guess again. You think that our lakes and ponds, rivers and streams belong to the people? You would be wrong. All fresh and natural water resources belong to the federal government under the auspices of the U.S. Army Corps of Engineers.

I have great respect for the military and the Engineers Corps. They have been foisted with a responsibility they did not seek. Now is the time to rectify that mistake and drop the law that places all water resources under the control of the federal government.

Problem, Response, Solution

Over the last 50 years or so, perhaps longer, a pattern seems to have emerged in the function and operations of the federal government. The federal government seems to be exploiting, and in some cases, causing incidents, that disturb American families or the health and wellbeing of the community. This exploitation seems intentionally designed to consolidate power and the wealth of the average American into the hands of the federal government. The federal government is a growing monster that is becoming more and more distant from Main Street America. What occurs within the Beltway has little to do with the way that average Americans live.

David Icke in his books has concluded that the U.S. government and several other governments around the world seem to have adopted a "problem, response, solution" pathology. This pathology seems designed to consolidate power and transfer the wealth of the people into the hands of big corporations and banks and bankers, (Bilderbergers?) and to make the average citizen dependent on the federal government for all their basic needs. If you must rely on the federal government for your daily bread and water, for the roof over your head and the clothes on your back and for your medicines and health care; you are much more unlikely to oppose the federal government in whatever it decides to do.

David Icke believes that authorities, in their bid to acquire power and subject people to their control, create a problem that initiates a cry from the people for the government to do "something" about the problem. The government then steps in with a prepared solution which solves the problem or at least puts salve on it, apparently, but which also, "incidentally" takes additional rights and responsibility away from the people and delivers these into the control of the federal government.

I concur with David Icke, at least in this area, although I disagree with some of his other conclusions. My own observation seems to indicate the same pattern of events and transition of wealth and control. People are becoming more dependent upon the government for their needs. My observations are occasionally astute.

From mid 1985 until January of 1986, I detected a pattern. Using solely public resources and media, I was able to conclude that a group was operating out of the basement of the White House and, using the CIA as a cover, was growing drugs in Iran for sale on the world market to fund the Contras in Nicaragua. I was also able to trace a Saudi Arabian, Israeli and South African connection. I was unable to place names and faces with this discovery, but in January 1986, the story broke. News media jumped on the "Iran Contras Affair" and Lt. Colonel Oliver North was seen as responsible for organizing and operating this clandestine group.

After 911, I detected another pattern involving the anthrax scare. Again, using only public resources, I was able to trace the source of the anthrax that journalists, Congressman and others were receiving in envelopes in the mail, to an Army lab in either Maryland or Virginia. I was able to detect a federal connection, perhaps within the FBI, but I was unable to determine whether or not this connection were the controllers of this operation or if they simply knew of it and chose to do nothing about it. Later the Army lab source was confirmed.

I mention these two incidents merely to highlight that, sometimes, I get it right, sometimes, I seem to detect a pattern where no one else does. And now, and for several years now, I have detected a pattern of operation by the federal government to consolidate power, strip Americans of their rights and transfer the wealth of the average American into the control of the federal government. I am unable to ascertain where the wealth is going, but it could be some organization of the federal government, the Federal Reserve, big banks acting in concert with the federal government or some force or organization behind the scenes or some combination of the preceding.

I would like to see an honest and open investigation into the true causes of 911, the anthrax distribution, TWA Flight 800 and KAL 007. There are other incidents but these four are a good place to start. I suspect the truth may be hidden behind and beneath layers of lies and misdirection, but perhaps not, perhaps they are all what the federal government claims they are what they seem.

Visitation: Business, tourism, educational and personal visits to the United States are extensive and varied. No application for a visa will be denied except upon clear proof of intent to commit terrorism or hostile action against the United States or citizens thereof. The time period of the visa shall be that which is necessary to conclude the activity so designated, but, for educational purposes only and only upon fulltime enrollment and attendance of an educational institute, may be longer than the average visa but never to exceed five years.

Green Energy: Environmental concerns are a serious issue. We cannot destroy the world which gives us life in order to maintain a destructive economy. We must find other means of energy; alternative energy sources, quantum energy, geothermal and solar are but examples. It is certain that the planet is undergoing climate change and is getting warmer. Although it seems that human interventions are not the primary cause, our industries and factories and millions of cars and trucks are a contributing factor. We must find an alternative. The federal government may be withholding alternative means of energy generation, but alternative means of energy generation are definitely needed. We cannot pollute the Earth to enable our way of life. If that were to continue, we would self-destruct and there would be no life. Inventors and researchers developing alternate energy sources should be funded and provided the best resources available. There are alternatives, some of them may already exist but simply have not yet entered the mainstream of public knowledge. We need to promote green energy and self-sufficient communities around the world. We should also seek to develop homes, factories, office buildings and retail centers that are self-sufficient in their energy needs. We can do it, it can be done, there is a way.

Health Reform: Part of the solution to health reform may be to establish a federally funded **free medical and dental clinic** in each community. This clinic would also provide vision services. This clinic would provide first aid, emergency care and on up to moderate levels of care. Some surgery and ambulatory care may be provided. Staffing could be part of the function of Armed Forces medical personnel.

I estimate each free medical clinic would cost between 175 million to 200 million to establish and 30 to 50 million annually thereafter to operate. I estimate the number of patients treated at between 10,000 to 20,000 annually.

A facility of this nature would tend to hold down health costs in each community it is located because of the nature of competitive markets. Only establishing one will ascertain how effective such a facility is in these goals.

The Last, Best, Great Hope of Earth: The United States has always been and shall always be, the Last, Best, Great Hope of Earth. The United States was built on principle and belief in an eternal Creator who has endowed humanity with certain unalienable rights. These principles and this belief is what drives the United States and makes us unique among the world. When the United States violates these principles, we diminish ourselves. When the United States commits action which violates this belief or said principles, all people of the United States and the world are hurt. The United States shall seek to restore these principles to the forefront of American policy, both domestic and international, and once again attain the light and hope of the world.

Hope, Peace, Happiness, Optimism and Love: The future is difficult, but it is not bleak, the future will be challenging, but not impossible, the future will test us, but it will not overwhelm us. We, the people of the United States have faced adversity before and overcome it, we have faced war and we have gained peace, we have faced injustice and wrought justice, we have faced financial meltdowns and built an economy second to none in the world. The present is difficult, so shall be the future. We will be tested, but we will not succumb. To create a better future for all of us, we must begin with collaborating with each of us. Though we may disagree on the methods, we do not disagree on our goals. We each seek a greater America, not a lesser America. We each seek a greater economy, not a weaker economy. We each seek a more responsible government, not an undisciplined, irresponsible government. We each seek a greener world, not an industrial world of constant pollution. We each seek a more responsible, happier and wealthier citizen, not a sickly, impoverished citizen dependent upon the whims of career politicians or an uncaring government. Although we differ on the role of government in pursuit of these aims, we do not differ on the aims. If we test numerous policies in state after state and community after community willing to accept such a trial, we can analyze the results and recommend a course of action. With the great polarization and dissension in America at this time, some may say this is too great, but America has always risen to such challenges. Some may say this is impossible, but with God, all things are possible. Others may say it can't be done, but Americans have always gotten it done. There is nothing we can't achieve, there is nothing we can't be, there is no dream we can't build, if we decide it will be. "Can't" is a word for those who get left behind by those who can, often time those who can are Americans. Americans understand that what we do is a result of what we are being and that what we have is a result of what we are doing. We understand that hard work coupled with a vision can turn our greatest dreams and aspirations into a tangible reality enjoyed by all. America has always been a nation of "can do," not "can't;" what needs to be done we will do, what is broken we will fix and what foundation the future requires is what we will build today. We will get it done, we will go forward, we are Americans.

Unity and Spirit: The world is an interconnected community in which all are one and one is all. Any action which hurts any being hurts us all. The physical world we observe is only a manifestation of and a tiny percentage of, the world of Spirit which undergirds and surrounds our existence. Not measurable by the tools of science, not comprehensible by the brightest mind, not observable by our most acute inspection, this world of Spirit is nevertheless a fact, a force which connects and unites each and every individual and bonds us with one another and the reality which surrounds us.

The American Dream: The American Dream is alive and well although it has suffered somewhat in the last several years. The American Dream is different for each person. The American Dream is this; that, supported by a freeing and stable government, an individual can, by vision and through hard work, attain any goal they have set out for themselves, live any life they have chosen to live and achieve any dream they desire. The function of government is to ensure that this is possible for each individual by getting out of the way of a person and their quest for the American dream and ensuring the government does not take away the self-responsibility of any individual, whether citizen, tourist, visitor, immigrant or student.

Why Government Programs Fail

The history of social programs shows that government must not be the organization that solves social problems, at least not in the way it has been. Government must only facilitate the individual to solve their own problems. The more problems government "solves," the bigger government grows, because there is no end to problems. The same is true for the individual. The more problems that person solves, the more that person grows. This is a goal to which all people should aspire. In solving more and more problems, a person becomes healthier, wealthier, happier, more effective, more intelligent and more sane.

Government cannot solve the problems of society because the problems of society do not reside in the government. A government that seeks to resolve any problem for any given sector of society only perpetuates that problem and makes that sector more dependent upon government. In addition, a sector so effected, becomes less and less effective, not only to itself, but to society as a whole. Each member of that sector participating in the government's program for solving the problem of that sector becomes more ineffective and more psychologically aberrated. This adds to the problem rather than providing a systemic method for the individual to attain improvement. We see then that the traditional social or entitlement program is ineffective at the problems it seeks to solve, perpetuates that problem and causes those people within the targeted sector to devolve into dependency and moral decline.

Exceptions do exist. Whenever an individual uses the program as a ladder to climb out of the problem state to a higher level of effectiveness and problem solving, the intent of the program has succeeded. The efficacy of any program must then be assessed by this metric. The continuation of any program should be based on a simple majority of the population within the targeted sector advancing out of the problem state to a more improved state. Any program which meets this metric should be continued. Any program which does not should be discontinued.

It can be further seen that those individuals climbing out of a problem state - by any means - are simply using those means to solve their own problems. Such individuals have accepted responsibility for their own circumstances and are simply using the means available to advance toward a more advanced state. These people understand that they are at cause for the circumstances and conditions of their life.

A condition of entry into any program can then be based on either of two criteria. The first is that any individual accepted into the program must understand that they themselves are the cause of their situation. The second is that any individual accepted into any program must immediately begin an educational series which educates the person into an understanding of their central role into the circumstances of their existence. A feature of each program must be a training course that instructs the individual how to resolve their own problems and advance into the next level of improved living.

Only with these conditions in place can any program actually be effective in any problems it seeks to solve. Without these conditions, any person advancing out of the problem state can be attributed to random chance or the ambition of the individual, not to any "inherent effectiveness" of the program. Programs must only be enacted which have these conditions as an integral part of the program. Only in this way can the problems of society be solved, individuals climb the ladder to their own success and society as a whole be improved.

THE MILITARY

Introduction

The United States Armed Forces provide for the defense and security of the United States and our friends and allies. Their primary purpose is, during peace, to deter war but if a war begins, to win it.

Our military services are noble professions with long tradition. The men and women who serve, our sons and daughters, our neighbors and friends are all dedicated to the security of our nation. They have set aside their lives and their families to serve, they have delayed work and business to fulfill a promise, they have replaced their own hopes for the dream of a better nation. Our service members come from every city and farm, they come from strong families and broken families, they come with insecurity and fear and with hope and strength. They are us, we are they, they deserve no less than the best we can provide, they deserve no less than our greatest respect, they deserve no less than our utmost admiration. These men and women, sons and daughters, neighbors and friends enter into service with the willingness to set aside a portion of their lives to build a better country and protect and defend their nation which holds so much promise. They enter the service knowing it will not be easy and that it will be hard, they know they must submit to strict rules and stricter discipline, they know that when they leave these lands for distant shores, they just may not return from the deserts, the mountains, the jungles or towns to which they have been sent. They know they may pay the ultimate sacrifice and yet they go willingly, with all this in mind. Our service men and women deserve the best we can offer, we can do no less.

The world is a dangerous place, suicide bombers and fanatics kill hundreds and thousands, dictators and generals lead their nations to war, warlords and criminals ravage cities and villages, rape women and burn villages, farms and homes. Into this fray we send our soldiers and airmen, into this destruction we send our Marines and SEALS, into the pit of death we send young lives. We are not always right in what we do, we are not always correct in the fights we choose, we do not always kill only those who would kill us. We make mistakes, commit errors and yes, some of our best even commit crimes. Yet all those who serve have one common connection, they are all Americans; they have one united goal, to defend and they share one great purpose; to end war and build peace.

In pursuit of our foreign policy, the military is often the instrument we wield to achieve our goals. When that foreign policy devalues human rights, supports dictators and overlooks wrong, we are doing a great disservice to our service men and women. I will discuss our foreign policy in more depth in the Foreign Policy section, here I will focus on our military.

We live in a multipolar world. We live in a global village, our trade and commerce crisscrosses continents and oceans, millions of people fly to thousands of cities around the world; our nation, our friends and allies, our rivals and enemies all compete for influence in an era of dwindling resources, constant war and never-ending threats to peace, life, trade and commerce. The goal of military force is to protect and defend the United States, our vital interests and our friends and allies from war and threat. In this complex environment, we must use our military judiciously to not only prevent war or win war when it comes, but also to promote peace, increase international stability and enhance global security.

All these aims are a daunting challenge to our leaders and the United States military. Yet it is a responsibility we cannot shirk, it is an obligation we cannot yield and it is a promise that we can not relinquish.

Preventing war is as important as winning war; winning peace is as important as preserving liberty. The United States has security interests around the world, we have international treaties to uphold and international obligations to fulfill; we have promises to keep and we will keep them. The United States seeks a world free of war and destruction, a world filled with hope and promise, a world of freedom and peaceful cities, villages, farms and homes. The United States is not the policeman of the world, nor should we be. The world has become too big and too complex with too many issues and too many interwoven arguments for any one nation to do it all alone. No nation can act unilaterally in all places, all locations, in all situations or for all causes. We must build and maintain a strong military, but we also must build and maintain strong alliances and strong friends.

The world has become increasingly complex, world commerce is becoming more and more tightly interconnected and interwoven; the drought that destroys crops and grain in one country can have affects around the world. The war in one nation can reverberate into every home. Into this complex mess, we often throw the United States military. Our Navy steams offshore distant lands to hearten our friends and discourage our enemies. Our satellites circle the globe to watch troop movements and observe facilities which may threaten us. Our drones cross the skies to watch, and sometimes strike, our enemies. Pirates raid commerce in distant seas, suicide bombers destroy lives in faraway cities, and religious fanatics threaten all. The United States must be vigilant and strong, we must be guided by a comprehensive vision and united in a common goal, we must seek peace, but be prepared to win war.

The Strategy of Peace

The Strategy of Peace is not a pacifist policy. The Strategy of Peace is an assertive strategy based on military and political power. Nations which employ a pacifist stance act the role of victim and soon become victims of more powerful nations. A nation employing a policy of strength has greater potential for ensuring its security, longevity, territorial integrity and the security of its friends and allies.

Underpinning the Strategy of Peace is a military truism: War is not about opposing armies, it is about the will of those who would send armies to war.

Utilizing this principle, the Strategy of Peace targets the will of the enemy leadership, convincing them that their initiation of hostilities would not only fail to attain their objectives, but would, in fact, be counterproductive to those objectives, to the entity or organization from which forces would be drawn and even to the leadership itself.

The Strategy of Peace is a simple strategy and consists of several steps:

1. Identify the enemy leadership - those who have decision-making power on whether or not to go to war.
2. Identify the organization. This could be a nation-state, political faction, regional coalition, a networked organization, terrorist pact or local gang.

   Each organization seeks survival and respect. There is no organization whose objective is self-destruction, although the destruction of the individual for the sake of the organization may be a valid principle for that organization.

3. Identify the motives and objectives of the organization and its chief players. What philosophy does the organization adhere to and/or seek to promote?
4. Identify the reasons and objectives the enemy entertains for hostile operations.
5. Search through all the data recovered and prepare a strategy which identifies the enemy's strengths and exploits the enemy's weaknesses while magnifying your strengths and neutralizing your weaknesses.

6. Prepare a fully orchestrated campaign utilizing all available channels of distribution to reach the enemy leadership and ensure that they receive your message.

The mass media, political analysts, think tanks, college students, social media, broadcast networks and talk shows, letters between corporations, husbands and wives, parents and students; multinational organizations, intelligence organizations, sports authorities and teams, et al, may all be contacted and/or employed (openly or surreptitiously) as a means to convey the terms of the Strategy of Peace to the enemy leadership.

This plan, the Strategy of Peace, will highlight and leverage Steps 7 through 9 below.

The message to convey to the enemy leadership must include the following points:

7. Convince the enemy leadership they cannot achieve their objectives if they do go to war.

8. Convince the enemy leadership that the material and psychological (to the mass body politick) costs of war to them will simply be too great from which to recover.

9. Encourage the enemy leadership that they may be able to attain the objectives they seek by going to war against some other entity.

Step 9, if successful, will serve to diminish the enemy's military capabilities reducing its ability to prosecute a war in the future. This may also serve to fracture the political infrastructure of the state and any such fractures must be exploited.

The Strategy of Peace is as applicable with guerrilla warfare, terrorist operations and gang activities as it is with nation-state operations.

National Security Strategy

American national security is a complex tapestry of interwoven parts and interconnected ideals. Our security is dependent upon the strength of our military, but is equally reliant upon our diplomats and politicians, our corporate leaders and university academicians, our legal systems and our intelligence community, our economy and our open markets, our productivity and our corporate competitiveness, our honesty and integrity, our democracy and transparency of government, our freedom and our liberty and our hopes and dreams. Our national security rests upon the quality of education we provide to our young, the research we support in our universities and think tanks and the entrepreneurs and businessmen and women who dare to create and build the products and services they feel will improve our lives. Our national security is dependent upon the moral character we hold not only as a nation, but that we also hold person to person. And all this is dependent upon our people. America is not a nation of brick and building, it is not a nation of field and forest, we are not a nation of wireless phones and downloaded apps; we are a nation of people. We are a nation of humanity from every shore, nation, race, religion and ethnic group around the world; we are young and old, male and female, strong and weak, bold and fearful. We are a complex people of diverse ideals, opinionated beliefs, strong wills and crude jokes. We a practical people and a whimsical people, we are the rich and the poor, we are healthy and we are not so healthy, we are religious idealists and pragmatic secularists, we are bold in vision and careless in wisdom. We are Americans. The world we seek to build, the nation we aspire to live in, the hopes we dare to believe, all are based on the security we feel protects us from our enemies, from crime, from fear and from encroachment into our lives by a megalithic, distant federal government. Our military has a role to play as do all the complex institutions of our lives, but most important is the quality of life we live as a people.

Holy Rights and National Security

The United States was founded upon the belief that there are certain things that are more important than life.

What is more important than life? Than living?

Some would argue that there is nothing more important than life. This is a common position of some communist ideologues. But even these communist ideologues, when pressed, would agree that their ideology is more important than life.

If life itself were paramount, than all else would fall by the wayside and wars would become meaningless. But life is not paramount and ideology is only one of several factors that are more important than life.

Wars are often fought on the basis of principle. Some of these principles include wealth, power and territory.

In the United States, our founding fathers and our traditions proclaim that human rights, universal democracy, freedom and liberty are all more important than life itself.

If the government shows compassion, caring and attention to the individual rights of the people; to fairness, to peace, to honesty, to integrity, to liberty, to democracy, to freedom; then we can be assured that the government is one in which the Principles of America are a function of the character of the government. But if these principles are excluded in the way the government functions; if we see no or little evidence of such principles in the daily activities and operations of the government, then we can be certain that the government is one in which only power and wealth have meaning.

Should the administration and the governmental apparatus under its control be found in activities which seek to preserve its wealth, power or security, then the Principles of America are being ignored by those who control the functions of the state. If the government resorts to torture, renditions, secret detentions, abuse or violation of the rights of any individual foreign or domestic, then the reins of government are held by those who believe only in power and wealth and the maintenance of their own position (security).

The government may claim such actions are necessary to protect national security, but what is "national security"?

If our nation was founded upon the principles of freedom, liberty, human rights and democracy with such rights innate upon each individual, then our nation is dependent upon maintaining and securing (security) these rights and principles for each individual.

Our nation's security (National Security) then is based on the government preserving, maintaining and where and when possible, expanding these rights for each person.

If the government fails to do this, it is not acting upon the basis of national security but only on the privilege and prestige of the rich and powerful - of those who lay claim to the functions of government.

Such a position is antithetical to a nation founded upon human rights, democracy, freedom and liberty for all. Such a position cannot be said to be "national security" but only the protection of those who seek to expand their wealth and power.

Is our nation protecting the rights of the individual which is true national security, or is it protecting only the power and riches of a few?

"Governments are mere machinery. It is the men who control them that count."
-unknown

"They that can give up essential liberty to obtain a little temporary safety, deserve neither liberty nor safety." - Benjamin Franklin

Decide for yourself. Analyze each administration. Weigh the actions of the federal government. Does it believe in the Principles of our Founding Fathers? The truth is revealed in the evidence. The evidence is the actions of government. Katrina, domestic spying and lies from the White House are all evidence. The passage of the Health Care Bill, bailouts of big corporations while the average person suffers and millions are out of work may also be symptoms.

You decide. What kind of government do we have? What kind do you want?

National Strategies

Other than my notes below, which just primarily reemphasize several points of these various strategies, I would make no other changes.

National Defense Strategy

1. Objective – The objective of the American military
    establishment is first and foremost, to protect the
    people and territory of the United States from all
    enemies, to secure and protect international lines of
    communication and commerce for all nations, to
    present American influence and provide for the
    security of allies and friends, to project American
    military force and power and provide for the
    successful conclusion of any engagement. When
    necessary, the military shall fight to preserve these
    tenets but only when the endgame is clearly
    defined, the necessary forces are assembled,
    adequately trained and equipped, senior military
    commanders are provided with clear instruction as
    to the politics and endgame and objectives and
    political leaders free the military to commit to battle
    and conclude the war without micromanagement
    from the political establishment.
2. War Policy – The United States shall herewith not
    intervene overtly or covertly in the internal affairs
    of any state which adheres to internationally
    accepted norms of freedom, peace and democracy.
    The United States shall not enter into war with any
    state without hostile action from that state. Hostile
    action may include, but is not restricted to, nation-
    state hostilities, state-sponsored terrorism or
    individual or group terrorism or hostilities. The
    United States will respond to protect and preserve

the lives, rights, assets and freedoms of the United States and American citizens wherever threatened.

3. Mission – The mission of the Department of Defense is;

    a. To properly prepare, equip and train our Armed Forces for war,

    b. To defend the nation and the American people against attack,

    c. To secure and protect international lines of communication,

    d. To project American influence,

    e. To aid and assist our friends and allies,

    f. To deter war,

    g. To win war.

4. Capabilities – To successfully complete these missions, several capabilities are required;

    a. To coordinate with contractors and vendors to supply the best equipment and services available,

    b. To ensure multiple suppliers remain viable and available for each item of equipment, hardware and software,

    c. To prepare and establish adequate training procedures and protocol,

    d. To optimize recruitment methods and coordinate recruitment activities,

    e. To establish efficacious command and control facilities and networks,

    f. To secure space and maintain defense satellites and spacecraft,

g. To prepare and win cyber warfare and conduct and coordinate activities with appropriate agencies in pursuit thereof,

h. To establish and assign functional service missions, areas of responsibility and unified commands,

i. To facilitate interoperability of communications, IT and intelligence regimens between the Armed Forces and federal agencies,

j. To cooperate with Departments of State, Commerce and other federal departments, agencies and international and civilian organizations as necessary,

k. To facilitate interservice training for officers,

l. To liaison with Congress,

m. To effectively communicate to the public the necessity, the functional capability and professional standards of the United States Armed Forces,

n. To maintain a fair and equitable military justice system,

o. To effectively plan for the current and future needs of the Armed Forces and the security and defense of the United States and its interests.

National Nuclear, Biological and Weapons of Mass Destruction Policy

The United States seeks a world free of nuclear and biological weapons and other weapons of mass destruction. It is recognized that this is an idealistic position and is unlikely to be achieved. Consonant with such a conclusion, the United States advocates a nonproliferation policy amongst world actors whether this be nation-states or nonstate actors.

The following will use "nuclear" in place of "nuclear, biological and weapons of mass destruction."

The position of the United States is to reduce nuclear threats, promote international disarmament and encourage nonproliferation. To achieve these aims, the United States will work closely with the United Nations Disarmament Agency, the International Atomic Energy Agency, international bodies and state and nonstate agencies and actors. Engagement is always better than hostile action and the United States will always seek, even if it must do so in private or through third parties, a comprehensive dialogue with those actors who possess or seek nuclear weapons or nuclear parity. As Winston Churchill once said; "jaw, jaw, jaw is always better than war, war, war."

The goal of the United States is first and foremost, to prevent the use of nuclear weapons. All other actions and positions derive from this goal.

The United States seeks to assure other nations and the world community that the nuclear arsenal of the United States is solely defensive in nature and serves only as a deterrent for the United States, friends and allies.

The United States seeks to ban the presence, stationing or use of nuclear weapons or fissile materials in space.

The United States will uphold international agreements and treaty obligations in regard to nuclear weapons and expects other signatories to do the same.

Our policy is to promote international agreements and treaties which restrict and reduce nuclear weapons and proliferation of nuclear weapons and materials.

We seek to assure friends and allies of the security of our weapons arsenal.

We further seek to assist and aid other nations in their weapons security even if such states remain outside of the Nuclear Nonproliferation Treaty.

The United States shall maintain a transparent policy in our nuclear decision-making and actions when and wherever it does not compromise national security.

We seek a moratorium on, or at least to reduce the production, sale and distribution of fissile materials and hardware and equipment that can be used in the production of nuclear weapons.

The United States supports international agencies whose role is to reduce nuclear proliferation.

The United States seeks to reduce the role and salience of nuclear power plants around the world and seeks to encourage alternate and advanced means of energy production.

Russia: The United States has maintained and will seek to continue a cooperative relationship in nuclear weapons policy and agreements with the Russian Federation. We further seek to move forward on bilateral agreements that reduce the nuclear arsenals of each nation. The United States seeks to maintain an open and effective dialogue with Russia to encourage international nuclear nonproliferation, reduction in nuclear weapons production and a moratorium or reduction in the production and distribution of materials and hardware that can be used in the production of nuclear weapons.

China: China is expanding not only its military strength and capabilities but is also expanding its nuclear weapons inventory and nuclear technology. This is a concern to the United States and we seek an open and honest dialogue with the Chinese leadership to accept international nuclear arms control agreements, in concert with Russia to ban nuclear weapons from space, to aid the international community in encouraging the nonproliferation of nuclear weapons and to help reduce international tensions whenever nuclear weapons are a concern. China has the potential to be a great friend and ally of the United States and world community and we seek to maintain and strengthen our relationship with China.

Iran: Iran presents a significant challenge to the world community in its apparent attempt to develop nuclear weapons. The stated objective of Iran that its sole purpose is to develop its nuclear regimen for peaceful purposes is suspect. The United States will promulgate a two-fold nuclear strategy with Iran: 1. To open a comprehensive, honest and transparent dialogue between Iran, the United States and the world community in regard to Iran's nuclear program and 2. To assure Iran's leadership that the United States is committed to the security and integrity of its friends and allies in the region and around the world and that the United States will not hesitate to deter the use of nuclear weapons on the part of Iran or to retaliate in kind by any use of nuclear weapons by Iran. The United States not only seeks peace, we seek to diminish the threat and proliferation of nuclear arms wherever that course may take us.

India: India is a growing ally and friend whose cooperation and relationship with the United States has been strengthening over the past decade. Although we seek India's acceptance into the Nuclear Nonproliferation Treaty, we will nevertheless work with India in the security of its nuclear arsenal if so requested. India and Pakistan have faced each other in military hostilities and the United States will seek to prevent the use of nuclear weapons by either state in the event of any future confrontation. The United States recognizes that India has a need for nuclear power generation and will not discourage India's use or development thereof except on the basis of international environmental threat if determined to be so by the international or scientific community.

Pakistan: The potential for disruption, distribution or use of Pakistan's nuclear arsenal is growing. As the state seems to slowly dissolve into instability, Pakistan's security of its nuclear weapons diminishes. The United States will closely monitor the security status of Pakistan's nuclear arsenal and will promote the development and improvement of Pakistan's nuclear security measures. Should Pakistan dissolve into chaos and its nuclear security be thrown into question, the United States reserves the right to act, in solo or in concert with other states or international agencies, to protect and secure Pakistan's nuclear weapons. In the event of war between Pakistan and India, the United States will seek to discourage the use of nuclear weapons by either state.

North Korea: As with Iran, the threat to world peace by the stated use of nuclear weapons by the North Korean government poses a serious challenge. The United States seeks to encourage North Korea to open an honest dialogue regarding its nuclear weapons and nuclear energy development with those nations North Korea feels it can trust. North Korea must feel certain that the United States poses no threat to its existence providing North Korea adheres to international norms and standards and nonuse of its nuclear weapons. The United States seeks a moratorium of North Korea's nuclear weapons research and production and its distribution of nuclear weapons hardware and fissile materials to other world actors.

National Military Strategy

The aim of the National Military Strategy is to support the goals and aims of the National Security Strategy and the National Defense Strategy.

Although the United States remains the world's sole superpower, the responsibilities of this power must be carefully and judiciously applied. Regional powers such as Brazil, India, Iran and China are rising. Russia is resurging; these powers will test American influence and our own and our partner's resolve. In most cases, there is plenty of room for all. The United States welcomes the rise of these powers and should seek to integrate and transfer some responsibility for regional peace and security to these rising powers. By engaging regional powers diplomatically, the United States should seek security sharing arrangements with each regional power. In cases where this would create a greater potential for tension in the region, the United States should retain its unilateral operations in this areas or, in concert with longtime allies or partners, share security and stability responsibilities for that region.

The Global Arena

The United States with the other states and nonstate actors in the world, recognizes a diversified world of challenging conditions, multiple resources and common areas of interaction. These common areas of interaction; air, space, sea and cyberspace, merit our attention and cooperation with others in the peaceful access, use, security and administration of these common regions. Criminal elements, pirates, terrorists, traffickers et al, all play a role in these areas. Hackers seek access and denial of service to networks and personal data. Pirates raid and hold hostage commerce on the high seas. Drug, human and restricted item traffickers seek markets for their illicit goods. Regional powers threaten international order and security. Failed states concoct plans to sell missiles and nuclear technology to rogue actors. All this, and more, are all examples of where the United States must take the lead in providing the right of access and use, to secure the peace and forestall conflict and to facilitate, where necessary, administration. The United States may not always be the lead actor in these areas. Wherever the United States is not the lead actor, the United States should cooperate fully and provide those resources available to those actors in the peaceful administration and access of said regions.

Mao Tse-tung wrote that military power is an extension of economic power. In order for the United States to maintain its Armed Forces at a level of strength and capability to meet our obligations and secure our interests, the prosperity of the United States must be the central area of focus. The military achieves this end by ensuring peaceful seas, open access, emergency aid, disaster relief and other forms of aid, administration, security and provision as able. We are not a sole power, we are not an imperial power; the United States seeks to share responsibility and cooperate fully with other powers in the world.

Partnerships with other nations and regional actors, including business and nonprofit organizations are vital to the security and prosperity of world commerce. The United States should seek to build on these partnerships and to generate additional partnerships. Only with friends and allies assisting in the security, access, use and administration of all these spheres of global interaction can the United States be effective.

The Arctic

The Arctic is evolving. Regional powers are claiming access and territorial rights. Natural resources are a function of this evolution. Global climate change promotes interest in the region by parties which had shown no interest in the past. The United States must act in concert with its partners and regional powers to assure the Arctic remains an open and free area of commerce and trade, that rights of access and transit remain open, free and available to all and that the environment of the Arctic is protected while natural resource extraction is undertaken.

Mexico

Mexico seems in a near state of civil war along the border region with the United States. Drug lords and criminal organizations violently vie for territory and control. Thousands of people have been killed in this violence. The

United States must increase its efforts to protect American citizens and territory from the spillover of violence and the extension of influence these threats represent. We expect to work and cooperate with the Mexican government to contain this violence and reduce the influence of the drug lords and criminal organizations in the area.

Caribbean and Central America

The Caribbean and Central America regions have been a relatively peaceful region although extreme violence and poverty manifest in some locales. The United States seeks a peaceful region with growing prosperity for all. The United States will not extend its customs or culture to this area, but will provide such security and aid as is necessary for the successful and peaceful evolution of this region.

United States Space Force – A United States Space Force shall be established to protect the right of the United States and its citizens and of all nations and entities the freedom of space operations as they see fit. No entity or nation has the right to adversely affect the operations of any other organization or entity in the conduct of its space affairs. All nations should respect the nonproliferation of nuclear weapons and weapons of mass destruction into space.

American Empire

There is no place in the world for an "American Empire." Today, this de facto American Empire exists sustained by over 700 U.S. bases and facilities in over 100 countries.

This forward presence is said to meet our strategic and national interests, but seems more in accord with forcing compliance by other nations and non-state players. The American way of life and democracy is not a "one size fits all" manner of being. Intimidating nations into accepting this American point of view is not in accord with the true principles of America or our way of life. A diverse world of different cultures, customs, religions, traditions and destinies create the multicolored fabric of human existence. The more diversified this fabric, the more rich our experience of living. We can enjoy the cultural differences and traditions of other nations and peoples without forcing them into an alien – for them – way of life, legal system or governmental structure. The majority of these bases and facilities are not necessary and an impartial panel should be commissioned to identify those bases and facilities which can and should be closed.

National Maritime Strategy

Seapower is the essence of maritime strategy. The United States possesses three services which function in the maritime realm. These services are the United States Navy, the United States Marine Corps and the United States Coast Guard. In pursuit of the goals of the Maritime Strategy, these three services must cooperate with each other in their operations and strategic focus. In order to achieve this aim, the United States should, under the auspices of the Department of Defense, establish a **Joint Maritime Task Force**. This Task Force will consist of senior members of each service and will seek to coordinate operations, assign activities and areas of operations, promote communication between the services, facilitate interservice training and promulgate interoperability of communications.

Seapower is broadly defined as the command and control of sea lanes of communication through the use of air, space and naval assets. The world is shrinking; global commerce increases and, in some locales, piracy and hostile states and nonstate actors present a threat to these sea lanes of communications. 90% of the world's commerce now transits by water and the lifeblood of nations moves over and across the seas. The oceans cover 70% of the world's surface and connect every major and significant world power. Rising world powers and the resurgence of Russia pose the potential to challenge U.S. and allied control of the seas and present the possibility of threat to the sea lanes. Regional powers exert influence over littoral waters and extend their reach and capability to nearby seas. The goal of the United States Maritime Strategy is to keep these sea lanes safe, secure and open to all nations. To ensure this goal, this Maritime Strategy includes provision for the training, procurement and operation of naval assets.

The United States Maritime Strategy encompasses six primary missions. These missions are:

To secure the sea lanes of communication.

To deter war and prevent or limit regional conflict.

To provide national defense in depth.

To win the maritime component of war.

To foster international relationships, strengthen alliances and assure allies.

To provide humanitarian assistance and disaster relief.

These missions are essential to the economic health and well-being of the United States and the global community, provide for the defense and security of the United States and friends and allies and contribute to world peace.

To assure the successful accomplishment of these six essential missions, several strategies must be employed:

Forward deployment,

Comprehensive training,

Adequate funding,

Effective procurement, recruitment and forward planning,

Enhance interservice interoperability, communications and integration,

Sufficient and comprehensive intelligence gathering and maritime domain awareness,

And,

Secure, clear and efficient chain of command and communications.

Notes –

Forward deployment

Power projection

Visibility – encourage friends, discourage enemies

Comprehensive training

And education – service academies, Naval War College

Adequate funding

Congressional liaison

Public interaction & awareness of maritime mission and essentiality (PR)

Commercial interaction and cooperation

Procurement, recruitment, planning

HQ

Officers' comprehensive and interservice and interagency exposure – training for all naval officers in the flag officer path should be exposed to the command, communications and operations of each of the other services. Perhaps a year, or at least six months service with each will provide the experience required for flag officers to effectively manage a diverse field of service elements and operational methodologies.

Interservice interoperability, communications & integration

Joint Maritime Task Force

Equipment interoperability – especially communications

Intelligence sharing

Joint training

Comprehensive intelligence gathering and maritime awareness

Space assets & satellites

HUMINT

ELINT

Movement of intelligence to comprehensive integrated interpretations – Although the compartmentalization of intelligence is critical for national security and operational security, a way must be found to consolidate the information gathered which now remains compartmentalized. A method must be established that brings all these disparate bits and pieces of intelligence data together in order for decision makers to get a clearer view of the "Big Picture."

Effective chain of command & communications

Officers training & joint service experience

Officers foreign naval attaché experience

Officers Congressional liaison experience

Streamlined, secure, integrated & concise communications protocol

Dual shipyards – The strategic importance of dual competing shipyards cannot be overemphasized.

325 Ship Navy

I feel that a minimum of 325 active major combat vessels are necessary for the U.S. Navy to fulfill the requirements of the National and maritime Strategies and meet mission objectives. Although I have broken out a fleet hull distribution below, this is only my guess. I am certain that the Admirals of the U.S. Navy have a much clearer picture of what ships of what kind are needed to fulfill the U.S. Maritime Strategy and meet mission objectives.

11 carriers

38 amphib warfare

50 attack subs

17 boomers

35 mine warfare

70 destroyers

55 frigates

32 cruisers

12 littoral

5 specialty (stealth attack)

China

China poses a real challenge and potential threat to the United States and other players in the western Pacific region. The U.S. Navy is meeting this challenge effectively, but I include my statement to stress the real and serious challenge China poses in this area.

China is claiming territory and islands to which it has no historical claim. From the Spratly Islands to its claim over the entire Yellow Sea and East China Sea, et al, China is walking a dangerous road. The Philippines indicate they will not relinquish their territory which China is claiming and they are willing to fight to hold onto it. Other states may take the same position. China's insistence that these areas rightfully belong to China presents the danger of conflict in the region. The U.S. Navy must diplomatically if possible, but with determination and without reservation strongly state the U.S. position regarding this area. These territories that China claims rightfully belong to the states currently in possession thereof and the United States will not tolerate any claim by China on these areas. The United States prefers a peaceful resolution to this situation, perhaps allowing China the right to access natural resources – particularly oil – that these areas may hold. If China should prefer force to claim these areas, the United States will, in concert with the nations involved, respond in like kind.

Taiwan

The mainland Chinese government claims Taiwan as a province of China. This is absurd. Regardless of the historical dimension of this situation, Taiwan is now and shall remain a free state independent of the central government of China. Again, the United States prefers a peaceful resolution to this matter, but if China should seek force to reclaim Taiwan, the United States will be obligated to defend. The United States Navy has been tasked to patrol this region and ensure freedom of the seas for all nations through the Taiwan Strait. In the event of hostilities, the U.S. Navy will be in the forefront of the defense of Taiwan. I would prefer a technology exchange between the United States and Taiwan which would permit the Taiwanese to upgrade their armed forces and build new capabilities, perhaps including cruise missiles. Until then, the United States may consider a loan of a few hundred cruise missiles to Taiwan along with Patriot missile batteries. We should upgrade our intelligence sharing with the Taiwanese military and consider allowing Taiwan our satellite intelligence plus the ability to request course corrections in satellite movements to overview Chinese facilities as the Taiwanese government may request. The United States should consider establishing a joint U.S.-Taiwan intelligence and communications center in Taiwan that will facilitate the collection and interpretation of mainland China's communications and intelligence data.

Naval Mission Specific Aircraft

Politics must not be a determinant in the aircraft the U.S. Navy, Marine Corps or Coast Guard receive. All aircraft delivered must be specific to the special requirements of fleet operations and naval missions and service requirements.

Terrorism

Killing the Snake - Defeating the Islamic Extremists

A counterinsurgency strategy is based on an understanding of the underlying causes of that insurgency. Attriting the existing members of that insurgency will not defeat the insurgency. Overturning the governments which seem to support or assist insurgency will not defeat the insurgents. In fact, both of these actions may radicalize those individuals not currently aligned or supportive of the insurgents and increase the number of volunteers available to the cause.

A primary underlying cause of insurgency is the ideology of those believing in the goals and aims of that cause. An ideology cannot be defeated with weapons or occupation of "enemy" territory; the weapons in play are ideas, the locations are every nation, city, village and home in the world, the environment is the mind.

One of the first acts in defeating a conventional enemy is to cut off the enemy's ability to communicate. This eliminates the ability of the enemy to control and command his elements in the field leading to disorganization and mislocation of those elements. This reduces the combat effectiveness and leaves those elements vulnerable to attack and elimination.

The act of cutting off the insurgent's ability to communicate may prove effective at a global level; the worldwide leadership, financial support and ideological recruitment on a mass scale would be eliminated. This will not eliminate local leadership, financial support or recruitment. These actions will continue regardless of how many "terrorist" nations are occupied or how many terrorists are killed.

Muslims believe that Islam is a superior ideology, it is not just a religion, it is a way of life which filters and colors every aspect of Islamic society. In the West, democracy is a form of government which separates religion from the state and empowers the individual over their leaders. Western women are not beholden to men, the people are not beholden to their leaders who govern and the faithful are not beholden to their clergy. In Islam, these roles are reversed. Democracy is a bottom up way of life, Islam is a top down modality. In democracy, control rests with the people, in Islam, control rests with the leadership. And that is the fundamental difference. It is also the key weakness.

The objective of a leadership is to conserve or expand their power; every contrary belief, ideology or government is a threat to that power and therefore must be addressed and vigorously opposed. The radical mullahs and imams are following this strategy exactly.

Around the world, the extremists are spreading their ideology of hate and vitriol. They shout slogans meant to inspire and enrage. They paint the western world as evil, with the leader of the western world - the United States – as the "great Satan". With the interconnectedness of the worldwide web, the radical extremists themselves are as deeply intertwined as a den of snakes is intertwined. Cutting their communications separates the snakes, but does not kill them.

Over the last several years, we have seen that one strategy to counter terrorism and aggression has been ineffective; to convince the enemy leadership that hostile actions on their part will spell their death. The mullahs and imams are convinced of their eventual success and are willing to die to achieve it. When one is captured or killed, another steps up to take their place, the ideology is not diminished, their war effort does not stumble, their funding is not impeded; their actions continue essentially unchanged.

We must find another means of leverage rather than the weapons of war and the hypocritical foreign policy we now follow. We must convince the Islamic leadership, all of them, that aggression against the West will spell the end if Islam. Alternatively, we must convince the leaders and the Muslim people that the true nature of Islam is to abide in peace and cooperation with other states and religions.

In Nazi Germany, Hitler's followers and war machine were constrained by geography; the geographical field of battle for radical Islam is the world. With Nazi leadership, there were a few who held power and maintained their ideology. With this power, they convinced their people that their worldview was accurate and factual. Using media and mass meetings they informed their people of the ills of their enemies focusing the attention and anger of their people against their enemy fanning the flame of their rage. The mullahs and imams are following this same strategy. Using mosques, madras, mass media and worldwide communications, the radical leadership convinces their people of the evils of the Western world. They convince people that the Western world's politics is evil, our economy is evil, our culture is evil, our foreign policy is evil, our disparate religions are evil and our liberalization of women and education are evil. These are points which cannot be easily countered as they appear accurate from one point of perspective. We can believe that our culture, politics and religions and the separation of church and state are superior, but from the point of view of the Islamic world, they are not.

Strategies for Defeating the Extremists

The extremists believe they are serving the wishes of Allah, they understand that Allah is the guiding force and principle that drives their ideology. With this single statement, we see the key to defeat the Islamic extremists.

There are two methods we can employ to win this war. Or, perhaps, we can employ both to some degree. The first is that, if the imams and mullahs believe Allah is their guiding force, is encouraging them and approving of their actions, (and they do) we must convince them that Allah is not. We must convince the extremists that Allah is opposed to violence, that Allah is opposed to the forced introduction of Islam into nations and communities that do not currently have an Islamic following and that Allah does not support the denigration of spirit or the continued illiteracy of the individual. Additionally, we must convince the radical mullahs and imams that Allah will punish those who support violence, radicalism and extremism in the name of Islam.

A second method is to educate, employ and advance the common Muslim into an understanding of a world that has no place for violence, destruction or hatred and to convince the everyday Muslim that a personal policy of peace, education, hard work, tolerance, entrepreneurship and honesty and integrity is the fastest and surest path to assure the achievement of the stated tenets and goals of Islam and of their own and their families benefit.

Islam is a great and peaceful religion which can peacefully and cooperatively coexist with other religions and non-Islamic states. This is the heritage and history of Islam and we must remind the Muslim people of this historical legacy of Islam.

In pursuit of method one, we must place doubt in the minds of those who lead and direct the extremist movement. We must position Western trained and/or progressive imams, mullahs and Islamic scholars in two positions in Islamic society. One position is as a key advisor to those who make the decisions. These people must be willing to sacrifice their lives and die at the hands of their own people or Westerners because their cover will be so deep, no one will know who they are. As key advisor, they should relay doubt on decisions and actions of the decision makers by asking "would Allah really approve?," by quoting surahs from the Quran which show an alternative to that decision, by identifying hadiths and historical actions which will benefit the cause of peace and by the continuous application of doubt about hostile actions and encouragement for peaceful actions.

The second position for these progressive individuals is within their communities. As university professors, doctors, lawyers, school teachers, local authorities, judges et al, the impact these progressive individuals can play in their communities can be substantial. Their influence will not only be contained within their community, but as their message filters out into the general population, it will eventually circle the globe. These progressive individuals must also view themselves as potential martyrs for a more peaceful world. As visible promoters of a progressive Islam within their communities, their safety and security can, perhaps, be addressed but not assured by Western military and intelligence actions.

In either case, identifiable contact between these individuals and any Western military, intelligence or even perhaps any Western person may compromise their position and undermine their influence.

In pursuit of method two, wherever possible, schools for the school age and training centers for those above school age should be established. The world has entered into a new economic period and the old style of economics has failed. A new style of personally integrated economics emphasizing personal financial responsibility must be established. Self sufficiency in homes and communities must be encouraged. Individual entrepreneurship must be encouraged. A job is no longer a guarantee of income and has never been a guarantee of future financial freedom or a source of individual empowerment. Literacy, Islamic and world history, mathematics and creative artistic studies must be encouraged in each school and training center. Islam must be encouraged to embrace the potential of the individual, not to suppress it.

Neither of these two methods will end this war overnight or even in a year or two. Both will take time and perhaps even a decade or more. In the meantime, we must protect our nation without abrogating our rights, encourage peace without sacrificing our principles and promote change without losing our heritage. The battle will not be easy but it can be won. This war will require persistence and determination perhaps over many years, but we won the Cold War, we can do it again.

A Global Problem, An Allied Response

Terrorism is a global menace. Bombs planted on subway trains in Spain kill hundreds, poison gas in a subway in Japan sickens dozens, a suicide bomber in a bus in London causes scores of injuries, a bomb goes off in Malaysia, the killed and injured number in the dozens; terrorists hold an entire school hostage in Russia, over a hundred children are killed. Terrorism in not a problem that exists only in a small nation faraway; it is here, it is now, it threatens us, our families, our friends and allies. Terrorism threatens our commerce, disrupts our business and damages our way of life; terrorism is not an isolated incident, it is a worldwide scourge.

To counter terrorism, we must meet with our friends, build relationships, strengthen alliances, integrate our intelligence gathering and coordinate our response. Terrorism is not a problem the United States can confront on our own, it will require a concerted effort between us and our friends and allies. We must share intelligence, improve our dialogue between our friends and agencies, build interoperability into our communications and develop a joint response.

Terrorists have no respect for borders or states, they have no respect for religions although they claim they do. The currency of the terrorist is violence, its payment is death and the frame is hatred. The terrorist seeks death and destruction; all who are opposed to their misguided policies and narrow ideals are their enemy. The religious fanatics of radical Islam seek the destruction of all that is Western; our nation, our communities and our lives are at risk. We stand under the threat of death and the destruction of our way of life. We are not alone, this threat extends to all people around the world, to men, women and children, to homes, businesses, public places and private locales across the globe. Our efforts must be focused, our determination relentless and our response quick, even and measured. With our friends and allies and the coalitions we build across national borders and beyond geographical boundaries, the threat of terrorism can be eased, reduced and eventually eliminated. It will not be easy, it will not be quick, it will not be simple. Defeating terrorism will require the cooperation of friends and allies and partners; it will not happen overnight, but with the help of God and the cooperation of others and the coalitions we build, it can be done.

POW's & "Harsh Interrogation"

Terrorist Prisoners – Terrorist prisoners are prisoners of war and will be detained under the auspices of the Geneva Convention with all the rights granted thereto. Prisoners of war are held until the conclusion of hostilities between the parties involved. Therefore, terrorist prisoners will remain incarcerated by the U.S. military until such time as the conclusion of hostile action is reached. Prisoners of war must be treated in accordance with the Geneva Convention and international treaties and obligations. At no time will the United States engage in "harsh interrogation" of prisoners whether alone or viscerally through third parties. Advanced modalities of interrogation were common and effective – and moral – until the advent of the Bush (George W.) Administration. The United States should continue these modalities at this time and into the future.

Renditions

"Renditions" – kidnapping of people off the streets and from their homes and businesses is illegal and must cease at once. Whether the U.S. acts alone, in concert with others or through third parties, renditions of all kinds must immediately cease. The policy of the United States must be to engage in no renditions at any time now or in the future.

Piracy

Piracy is an act of war committed by individuals against seagoing vessels and commerce. The United States shall instruct the United States Navy, Marine Corps and Coast Guard to maintain a presence in known areas of pirate activity thereby to destroy without recourse any and all those caught in the act of piracy. Those who are captured without being caught in the act of piracy and are suspected of such actions will be classified as terrorists.

UFO Policy and High Technology

British historian Arnold Toynbee in his seminal work, "A Study of History," reached the conclusion that contact between an inferior civilization and a superior civilization always results in the destruction of the inferior civilization. I concur with his conclusion. This theme may, perhaps, be outdated and obsolescent due to the advancing technology and greater sophistication of our civilization, but I see no evidence or indication that any contact between said societies should warrant the risk of such public contact.

I believe in UFO's. I believe in aliens, alien technology and extraterrestrial civilizations. I also believe our government has recovered UFO's and has reverse engineered the technology from such craft. I believe the United States has an operational, but secret, "Star Wars" type program and that contact between the U.S. government and alien entities is ongoing. I do not believe this information should be made public at this time. The threat to society is too great in accordance with the findings of Toynbee. I feel the U.S. government may be engaged in a type of progressive revelation of the existence of aliens and alien technology, in which bits and pieces of the puzzle are "leaked" and them immediately publicly discredited by the same sources releasing the material. I concur with this policy and feel it should continue. This policy, if indeed it exists, seems to be effective in slowly educating and raising public awareness in the possibility of the existence of extraterrestrial civilizations.

We see TV shows, cable TV shows, Hollywood movies and books and blogs all expressing this theme of UFO's and advanced technology in some way. The public seems to be coming around to accepting and acknowledging the possibility that we are not alone in the universe. I feel NASA and other sources need to accelerate this trend. The next step could be to release or "leak" information regarding the "recent discovery" of microbial organisms on Mars or the existence of interspace non-intelligent biological entities. A further step would perhaps be to release or leak information regarding the "inconclusive" possibility of the identification of artifacts of a long dead civilization on the Moon or Mars. I feel these measures, and others like them, would accelerate the public and world acceptance of extraterrestrial civilizations to the point that, within a few years, the world will accept without extreme disquiet or trauma the public revelation of the existence of UFO's, alien technology and extraterrestrial civilizations.

High Technology

The existence of advanced technology derived from reverse engineered alien technology and/or in-depth research into the writings of Nikola Tesla may be a fact. That our nation and human civilization has made extremely rapid progress in technology within the last hundred years cannot be denied. It is unfortunate that our social progress has not kept pace. Research projects and studies conducted over a number of years by such entities as DARPA, U.S. Naval Intelligence, United States Air Force, the Soviet Union – and now the Russian Federation, Lockheed Martin and Boeing, amongst others seem to have identified, extracted and successfully developed certain aspects of advanced technology whether or not such technology is directly derived from alien sources. HAARP, scalar technology and physical systems may all be derivatives of this research. To the extent the U.S. government is knowingly and willingly engaged in actions and projects which endanger the American population and world society and puts our physical world at risk, these projects must be curtailed immediately. Whether it be HAARP, weather control or at-distance scalar influence of subject demographies, et al, these initiatives are a violation of human rights, United States law and the Constitution. The U.S. government has no authority to subject the American people or the world to endangerment or physical injury from high risk activities. Continued research into stealth technologies, advanced communications systems, exotic propulsion designs, quantum energy derivatives and other high technologies – which do not endanger or risk public health – must continue. The universe is a very large place, projects underway will shrink this expanse to a scalable dimension making human progress and travel to other systems and interaction with other entities possible and, eventually, common. The office of the President and the appropriate committees of Congress must encourage, guide and fund these initiatives for the good of all mankind and, when appropriate, release the results of this research into the hands of the public.

Alien Invasion

If aliens were going to invade, it probably would have happened long ago. I am detecting early indications that the federal government may be preparing a "false flag" operation regarding an alien invasion. This would be a false invasion coordinated behind the scenes by federal authorities. The sole purpose of this "invasion" would be to further strip Americans of their wealth and rights and consolidate power and control to the federal government. Whether this is accurate or not, only time will tell. But if said "invasion" does occur, we must look with skepticism to its origin and controlling influences. It may be real, but it could be – and probably would be – a false flag operation.

Foreign Policy

The United States does not exist in a unilateral world. A global, multi-polar world has grown all around the United States and the United States must seize the initiative to be the leader of the global community. This requires commitment to international norms of behavior, adherence to the rights and principles of the Constitution and the Declaration of Independence and establishing open lines of communication with allies, friends and foes alike. No longer will the United States support dictators and totalitarian regimes in countries whose sole benefit to the United States is their resources, strategic position or influence with their neighbors. Support for any such states or leaders, whether overt or covert, shall be terminated.

Our foreign policy must be consistent with our stated aims and goals, with our principles and with international law and order and seek to preserve and expand international security and stability. The United States will be unable to achieve these aims when our foreign policy upholds dictators who deny human rights to their citizens; when we contradict our own laws and principles in our actions and when we overlook wrongs when we should be making things right. The offenses of our past are no excuse for pretenses in the present. We must admit our mistakes, fix what is broken, right what is wrong and move forward boldly while maintaining our rights and principles. The United States admits it errors in our foreign policy in past administrations. We cannot change history but we can work in the present to assure a consistent, fair and peaceful foreign policy. The mistakes of our past have produced enemies and antagonists that threaten the American people, our interests and commerce. All threats are considered serious provocations of the peace. The United States shall take such steps as are necessary to forestall any such threat. We will seek to establish a dialogue with transitional forces to address the legitimate grievances these entities may harbor against the people, government or interests of the United States.

Nuclear Proliferation – The policy of the United States shall be to prevent states from acquiring nuclear weapons. It is understood that states have a need for self-defense as well as a need for energy. The United States supports the Non-Proliferation Treaty and supports the introduction of nuclear power plants into any nation which deems it necessary to introduce them. The objective of the United States is that the most efficient, green and technologically advanced power plants are desirable. Several states possess nuclear weapons. These weapons must be kept safe and secure from all threats from within and without that nation. If necessary, to protect these weapons from falling into the hands of terrorists or international criminal organizations or entities, the United States reserves the right to act unilaterally to secure these weapons. Fissionable materials and nuclear waste currently in existence and that which may be generated by future activities must be secured and adequately disposed within the highest international standards.

Green Energy – Global warming threatens the existence of humanity. Though scientific surveys and advisers may disagree, it cannot be discounted that carbon gasses in the atmosphere pose a threat to the environment and may already have done nearly irreparable harm. Therefore, the objective of the United States shall be to promote green energy in any way possible within fiscal responsibility. This shall hold forth regardless of the state or organization researching or providing said technology.

International Infrastructure - The United States supports 100% complete self-sufficiency in each community, urban area, residence and facility and shall seek, encourage and promote all research and activities to secure such promise. Medical facilities of appropriate scale and educational facilities with programs in consideration of the customs, culture and history of the location shall be maintained. In addition, those which provide education in world history, democratic process and moral and immoral capitalism and other economic forms shall be provided. Individual farming, household water management, facility waste management, home energy sufficiency and other programs as identified which promote and provide individual and household independence and self-sufficiency apart from centrally organized networks shall be established and researched. Highways, dams, railways and other transportation modes shall be encouraged to promote interdiversity, education, economic progress, the democratic process and facilitate integration of worldwide tolerance.

Ocean Fishing – Worldwide fisheries are becoming exhausted. Continued overfishing will deplete the replenishment of fish within their fishing banks. The United States shall support a worldwide rotation of states undertaking fishing within common fisheries. In addition, the United States shall introduce to the United Nations legislation that creates an organization which regulates "ocean ranching." As in the Old West of the United States, research shall be undertaken until a solution is discovered permitting the operation of fishing ranches worldwide. These will operate by providing safety and security to breeding populations of seagoing creatures, feeding them and then harvesting them at maturity at which time the cycle will renew.

Whaling – Cetaceans are intelligent creatures. No research can be done on any intelligent creature without that creature's assent. If there is no communication between you and that creature, there is no assent. If there is communication but that creature does not understand or does not agree, there is no assent. Whaling is illegal, the United States shall protect to whatever degree whales from being slaughtered by any nation by any means necessary.

The Internet – The objective of the United States is a worldwide internet free of governmental restriction or control of any kind by any nation. An unfettered, free and open internet in each and every country is the objective of the United States. As such an unfettered, free internet will encourage the illegal action of individuals exploiting children, pornography, identity or monetary theft and fraud or crimes, the United States shall promote the ability of each state to investigate, capture and prosecute each activity as that state shall deem fit. The restriction of the internet is not permissible in the view of the United States and the United States shall actively pursue the openness and freedom of the internet in each and every state, but also encourage each state to justly uphold and enforce its own laws within international stated parameters.

Economics

A global economy cannot be denied. The reality of each state intertwined economically with all others is a current and future state. The objective of the United States is to encourage the growth in the economy of each nation and state, the promotion and introduction of capitalism to each nation of the world at a time and manner suitable for that nation and the establishment of capitalism unique to the culture, history and customs of that state.

The immorality of uncontrolled capitalism cannot be denied as the Robber Barons of the United States 19th and early 20th centuries attest and as the Enron's, Bernie Madoff's and Wall Street bonuses at the expense of Main Street America of current times attest. The United States shall propose new legislation both internationally and domestically which bears real teeth for any grievance of illegality. This proposal shall include - upon complaint, investigation, justification and warrant - immediate seizure and impoundment of all a corporation's assets and facilities, immediate cessation of all activities, immediate imprisonment of all executives and replacement of executives with federal agents thoroughly trained and certified in corporate management and operations. Executives shall be released from imprisonment only upon completion of filing of appropriate charges and presentment of bail as ordered. Corporations so seized shall be returned to operations under federal management as soon as conditions permit but within 24 to 48 hours whenever possible. Future disposition of such corporations shall remit to legislation and may include continued operations with no further action, sell-off of assets or other restructuring as may be determined.

Capitalism – A new form of capitalism must be devised. The capitalism of the past has failed. The greed and immorality inherent within the human heart comes to light within a capitalist (or even socialist, fascist or other) system. A prosumer, individual approach to financial capability must be established. The United States shall seek to establish in each worldwide urban area a school of capitalism that teaches this new form of capitalism to all students. This new form of capitalism must take morality, spirituality, individualism and care for others, amongst other items, into consideration. Individual savings, individual self-employment, individual financial independence, individual self-sufficiency and individual green living are all tenets of the new capitalism.

World Bank and IMF – The World Bank and the International Monetary Fund are prime examples of the misdirection of the old style of capitalism. These institutions must be restructured to secure true rewards for the people of the area in which economic progress and peaceful modernization is the objective. This restructuring must include the tenets of the new capitalism.

Democracy – The policy of the United States is to promote and encourage democracy in each and every nation. The mode of democracy must be unique to that state with consideration of the culture, history and customs of the people of that state. The United States shall promote the peaceful integration of democracy within each state at a rate that state shall deem appropriate. The United States shall not seek to enforce or require any state to accept the United States brand of democracy except that the rights of each person shall be respected as well as the one person, one vote, openness of the democratic process, transparency of government and freedom of political parties, philosophy of democracy shall be maintained.

The Strategy of Peace – This initiative is the modus operandi of the United States; to avert war, we must prepare for war; to ensure peace, we must be assertive in our policies, to be a leader, we must be adamant in our principles. We will conduct our international relations in accordance with this policy because it presents an understanding of the human control of nation-state and group hostile actions committed upon others. To secure peace, the United States must not only be assertive, it must also understand the mind of those who would call for war or aggression against the United States or its citizens.

Intelligence Policy – To prevent war, the United States must be prepared for war. To prepare for war appropriately requires that the United States secure accurate information regarding the actions and plans of any potential adversary. This accurate information may be gathered in modes which the United States deems necessary and appropriate to achieve its goals including that of covert action and covert surveillance. Any and all information gathered must remain secure and classified for a sanctioned interval of time.

Natural Resources – Natural resources are a worldwide commodity controlled by a state or several states. The right of each state to control its commodities as it sees fit within international norms shall not be restricted. United States policy shall be to allow nation-state control and administration of its natural resources as long as such management does not adversely affect world affairs or economic progress.

International Space Command – The United States shall seek an International Space Command organized under the auspices of the United Nations to provide for the training, access and exploration of space for all nations. Planet Earth is becoming overcrowded and resources are depleting while an inexhaustible supply of resources and living space exists just a few hundred kilometers overhead. The peaceful and green exploration and development of space shall be the goal and purpose of this organization. Headquarters of the International Space Command will be made available, perhaps utilizing the former Presidio of San Francisco.

Russia – The United States policy goal is to establish and maintain Russia as a true, strong and valuable ally of the United States. The United States and the Russian Federation experience conflicting goals and methods regarding some areas of concern. The United States understands that Russia must act in its own best interest while the United States does the same. Although the United States and Russia may oppose each other on some issues, that is no cause for the dialogue between our two nations to be adversely affected. The Russian military is growing and building and extending influence, once again, throughout the world. The United States should welcome these efforts and seek to share responsibility for peace, security and stability with Russia in areas in which Russia possesses greater influence than the United States. Although we will monitor Russia's expansion of its armed forces and the increase in its military capabilities, we see no cause for alarm nor do we consider such actions a threat. In the event this process reaches a point of contention, the United States will initiate a dialogue with Russia on these issues and seek a peaceful, mutually acceptable resolution. It is our belief, that cooperation between our two nations can provide a high level of benefit and trust to each state.

Vietnam – We seek a rapprochement with Vietnam. To serve that end, the United States shall initiate and promote continued communications with the Vietnam government, joint operations with its military and an engagement with the commerce and democratic process of the people of Vietnam. The United States shall, upon request, station troops along the Vietnamese-Chinese border to preserve the territorial integrity of the state of Vietnam. The objective of the United States is a peaceful, open Vietnam with a movement toward the new capitalism and democratic process.

Cuba – Fidel Castro has stated that the communist form of economics has failed although the Revolution lives on. The Revolution that Fidel speaks of is that which condemns the immorality and greed of the old (current) capitalist model. The United States sees no reason to dissuade this viewpoint. We hope that Cuba will transition peacefully and integrate fully into the world community, respecting the human rights of its citizens and assuring an open and free press and an open and transparent government. Should a request be presented, the United States will respond as appropriate.

China – China is a strong and stable ally in East Asia. We must find ways of cultivating that relationship while maintaining our liberty and security and the liberty and security of other nations and territories in the area.

      a. With this in mind however, we note the increasing aggressiveness and imperialist tendencies of China. The United States will seek to thwart these tendencies in ways that promote peace, liberty and security of the region while protecting and enhancing the natural rights of all people. We will applaud every effort of China to expand and extend democracy in their own land and we will condemn every reversal or diminution of this. We fully expect China will apply this same policy to the United States.

b. Tibet: The Office of the President of the United States privately acknowledges that Tibet has been part of China for many hundreds of years. We have no idea where the propaganda of a free Tibet originated or what purpose it serves. Having said that, we support the Dalai Lama in his efforts at peace and stability and for the integration of Tibet into the world community. Publicly, the United States will support the call of a free Tibet but shall not act to make this a reality, except that we reserve the right to meet and interact with the exiled Tibetan government headed by the Dalai Lama.

c. Stealth: We hereby acknowledge that China possesses stealth technology that may equal or exceed the United States' own stealth capabilities. We understand that China is in possession of stealth missiles, aircraft and submarines the United States cannot currently detect. Any intrusion into United States, Canadian or Mexican airspace or any violation of territorial integrity, whether land or sea, of any three, will be considered an act of war and specific measures to counter said threat shall be undertaken.

d. Commandos: Chinese commandos, special operations forces and military, paramilitary or terrorist personnel violating the airspace or assuming a presence on the ground or sea within the United States, Canada or Mexico will be considered an act of war. The United States hereby authorizes the use of lethal force. After the first warning and return of surviving prisoners to China, no prisoners shall be taken.

e. Any attack or destruction of United States equipment, materials, disruption of supplies or death of United States citizens whether military or civilian whether in or over the United States or territories or allies thereof or any third country or international or spatial region where the United States maintains a presence, will be countered with equivalent and direct force.

f. Taiwan: The United States is a friend and ally of Taiwan. Any threat to Taiwan by China will be countered, any attack will be countered and every attempt to thwart the special relationship the United States maintains with Taiwan

will be countered. If China wants
Taiwan, they must fight us for it.

g. Pacific Friends and Allies: The
territories of the United States and the
friends and allies of the United States
throughout the Pacific and Indian Ocean
region are under the military protection
of the United States.

h. Freedom of Religion/Christianity: The
United States seeks to promote freedom
of religion within China. The assault of
churches and believers, destruction of
churches and meeting centers, arrest,
detention and torture of attendees at
services has been duly noted. The United
States condemns such action. Upon
request and whenever possible, the
United States will support and donate
materials, funds and supplies to the
establishment and maintenance of any
religious center or organization so
requesting.

i. Freedom of
Assembly/Protest/Demonstration/
Redress: The right of any and all human
beings to meet and protest, demonstrate
for or against a cause or their
government, to petition their government
or elected or public figures for redress of
grievances, to seek equitable justice by

or from their government or public officials and to associate with one another shall not be denied, prohibited, interfered with or prevented by China, as assessed by the United States or appropriate world body, and will not be condoned by the United States and may be met with an action of condemnation, sanctions or other action as is deemed necessary and appropriate by the United States.

j. Freedom of Speech/Press/Internet: China's sometimes subtle and sometimes open and aggressiveness hostile action against its own citizens seeking these rights and the use of these measures has been noted. The United States shall not condone any action when observed.

k. Cyber Warfare: The increasingly aggressiveness and hostile actions by China against the United States and the world community has been duly noted. Each and every hostile action by China in the cybersphere shall be considered an act of war and countered with equal force.

North Korea – North Korea is waiting for reunification. We must push for that reunification with South Korea as soon as possible. The United States will seek to restrain and prevent North Korea from violating the peace, liberty or security of its neighbors or of the world. If possible, a dialogue should be established to help bring order and peace to the two Korea's.

A pariah in the world community, North Korea's exports of missiles, missile technology, arms and nuclear technology to other parties is a grave and serious concern. We seek a moratorium on North Korea's nuclear ambitions and arms exports. We seek a peaceful transition of North Korea and hope for a peaceful integration of North Korea and South Korea into one unified state, at peace with the world, with respect for human rights, prosperous and growing. This may not be possible any time soon, but the United States will continue to work with South Korea and other world and regional powers to facilitate this unification.

South Korea – Our great friend and ally is a state which has prospered in the last two decades or so. A growing economy, the engine of manufacturing, a happy and peaceful people, democracy and a free press for all combine to create one of the most successful nations in history. Across the Demilitarized Zone lies North Korea, a state still technically at war with the south, an antagonist and disrespector of human rights, its aggression and hostile actions against the south are a disservice to the world community and threaten the peace and security of the region. 30,000 U.S. troops guard the border and our Navy and Air Force patrol the sea and airspace. We stand ready to aid South Korea in any attack upon it by the north and will not hesitate to commit our Armed Forces to repelling any such attack.

Japan – Our ally Japan has been aligned with the US and with US interests since the end of World War 2. Following a carefully executed economic policy with the quality control standards of W. Edward Deming and a manufacturing process copied from the US, Japan has been a shining example of what many nations can aspire to. Japan's economy is uniquely Japanese, highly capitalistic and free flowing. Although there are problems, there are no problems which the Japanese cannot handle on their own.

Asia – The nations of East and South Asia are the fastest growing economies of the world. Each uniquely their own, each is also a member of the growing world community. We must assure the unfettered progress, growth and integrity of each of these while it lives in peace with its neighbors, its own population enjoys the enhanced wealth of a world economy and the world benefits from the culturally diverse natures of each entity. The United States will promote peace and stability throughout Asia and act in concert to build successful communities, prosperity and peace.

Europe – The nations of Europe are the ancestral home for the vast majority of Americans. The United States is close allies with or friendly with nearly all nations of Europe. The nations of Europe are all generally democracies, each with their own particular flavor of democracy. The United States recognizes several European states as strong allies and will seek cooperation and coordination in areas of mutual interest with all European states.

Africa – Africa is a great, historic and beautiful continent of majestic scenery, rich history and enthralling culture. Many nations exist on the African continent, some of which are friends or allies with the United States and some of which are not. Each nation shall be treated in due measure with the full consideration of its relationship with its people, its role on the world stage and its association with the United States. The United States shall respect the diverse cultures, history and rich traditions of the states of Africa and appreciates the rich diversity these nations provide. The United States recognizes the famine and poverty of some areas of Africa and we seek, working in concert with our partners in the region, to provide assistance and aid as possible. The United States also recognizes the violence and hostility within regions of the continent and shall work with other states and partners to ameliorate these conditions and provide aid, assistance and security as possible. The United States seeks self-sufficient communities and will aid efforts to transition communities into peaceful, self-sustaining communities.

Venezuela – We have no quarrel with the people or government of Venezuela. The United States recognizes that each state has the right to conduct its own affairs as it sees fit and to govern in a manner that is consistent with their cultures and traditions as long as the government respects human rights and adheres to international norms and standards.

Iran – Iran is a clear example in which the United States has no quarrel and harbors no ill toward the people, but has serious concerns regarding its government. We do not seek a quarrel with the state of Iran, but require that the government of Iran respect human rights within its own territory and fulfill its international obligations. The United States will not tolerate hostile actions by the government of Iran toward any other party nor will we allow any such actions to occur without a firm response. The United States expects that the government of Iran will assure the peace and security of the region, assure world commerce and freedom of access and use for all parties throughout the Gulf region. The United States will view any threat by the government of Iran against Israel, any of the Gulf states or any friend or ally of the United States as a real concern and shall view any such threat as a potential for conflict.

Canada, United Kingdom, France, Germany – The United States works extensively with each of these states to secure world prosperity and security, provide access to resources and educational systems, extend aid to other nations and promote peace, security and stability throughout their areas of proximity and throughout the world. We expect our special relationships with each of these states to continue and the United States will seek to cooperate, coordinate and assist in any such areas as may arise.

CONCLUSION

The United States is a great nation with diversified communities and diversified interests. We have great and unique responsibilities throughout the world, yet we cannot function in solo. We depend on our friends, allies and partners for the security, stability and peace in the world and we will not hesitate to facilitate that peace and security whenever possible. We seek to work in concert with our partners and international organizations to build a more peaceful and prosperous world. Although the United States feels its system of capitalism, (the new capitalism), democracy and reformed government is best and we feel it would serve every state and region, we recognize the impracticality and error in worldview of such a sentiment. We are a proud nation of diverse peoples and we recognize our role in the world is unique.

The United States may be experiencing difficulty at this time in government, in our economy and in our vision of our role in the world. Although we may disagree amongst ourselves on methods and modalities, we do not disagree on our aims; to build a greater, more prosperous nation with greater freedom and liberty and we seek the same throughout the world community. It is through peace that prosperity grows and we will seek peace whenever possible. We recognize however that there are enemies and others who oppose our worldview and that of the world community. We further recognize that these may be states, nonstates, failed states or organizations. The United States will not shirk its responsibilities in the world or at home and we are prepared to fight for our beliefs, our security and our happiness.

The United States is the world's sole superpower. "With great power," so the maxim goes, "comes great responsibility." We understand that our power must be used fairly and judiciously not only in the far corners of the world, but also in the streets of America.

--- --- ---

We the People, ... hold these truths to be self-evident, that all men are created equal, that they are endowed by their Creator with certain unalienable rights, that among these are life, liberty and the pursuit of happiness. That to secure these rights, governments are instituted among men, deriving their just power from the consent of the governed. ... That government of the people, by the people, for the people, shall not perish from the Earth. And, .. with a firm reliance on the protection of Divine Providence, we mutually pledge to each other our lives, our fortunes and our sacred honor. May God help us all.

158

INDEX

INDEX

INDEX

INDEX

INDEX

INDEX

INDEX

PERMISSIONS